George Colman

Prose on Several Occasions

Accompanied with Some Pieces in Verse

George Colman

Prose on Several Occasions
Accompanied with Some Pieces in Verse

ISBN/EAN: 9783744685832

Printed in Europe, USA, Canada, Australia, Japan

Cover: Foto ©Thomas Meinert / pixelio.de

More available books at **www.hansebooks.com**

PROSE

ON

SEVERAL OCCASIONS;

ACCOMPANIED WITH

SOME PIECES IN VERSE.

BY *GEORGE COLMAN.*

VOL. I.

*—— Seu me tranquilla senectus
Expectat, seu Mors atris circumvolat alis,
Dives, inops, Romæ, seu fors ita jusserit, exul,
Quisquis erit vitæ, scribam, color.——* Hor.

IMITATED.

Whether Old Age a tranquil evening brings,
Or Death sails round me with his Raven Wings;
Rich, poor; at Rome, or London; well, or ill;
Whate'er my fortunes, write I must and will.

LONDON:
PRINTED FOR T. CADEL, IN THE STRAND.
M DCC LXXXVII.

TO

SIR JOSEPH BANKS, BART.

PRESIDENT

OF THE

ROYAL SOCIETY,

DEAR SIR!

TO offer to You, who are manifeſtly engaged in the moſt uſeful and moſt reſpectable ſtudies, a Collection of Fugitive Pieces, may perhaps at firſt ſight appear to the

VOL. I.   A   world

DEDICATION.

world as a flagrant impropriety, or at beſt but an ill-timed compliment.

But the truth is, it is not my deſire to ſhelter theſe Papers under the Patronage of the PRESIDENT of the ROYAL SOCIETY; but to ſeiſe this opportunity of publickly teſtifying the ſincere reſpect and regard I entertain for your Character, and to acknowledge the Obligations that I owe to Sir JOSEPH BANKS.

Theſe conſiderations will, I truſt, be received as an Apology by the Publick, and will, I hope, induce You to pardon the liberty I have taken in requeſting

DEDICATION.

requesting your friendly acceptance of these little volumes, as a faint pledge of the Veneration and Gratitude of,

Dear Sir,

Your most obliged

And most faithful

Humble servant,

Richmond,
April, 23, 1787.

GEORGE COLMAN.

PREFACE.

DRIVING the other day through the City—*driving*, for alas! at prefent writing I cannot very well walk—I obferved, in different panes of the extended window of an eminent Linen-Draper, a confpicuous Bill, exhibiting thefe words in very large Characters: THE GOODS OF THIS SHOP TO BE SOLD CHEAP, THE OWNER LEAVING OFF TRADE.

Though it is not my intention to fhut up Shop, and though I fhall not probably leave trade till life leaves me, yet meditating at that moment on the few pages neceffary to be prefixed to thefe Mifcellaneous Volumes, I could not help comparing my Stock of Effays, Prefaces, Letters, Remarks, Odes, Epiftles, Epigrams, Prologues, and Epilogues, with other Literary Fragments, to the

the Bales, Pieces, and Remnants, of my frriend the Linen-Draper.

In one refpect indeed our fituations are exactly fimilar; we are both obliged to evacuate our feveral warehoufes, and though we may both on this occafion bring forward fome ftale commodities, yet we both offer all our prime goods much below prime coft.

Nay, fays a Critick, but your cafe and that of your friend are not, as you pretend, exactly fimilar. He is under a neceffity of difencumbering himfelf of all his wares, good, bad, or indifferent; but from you we have a right to expect and demand a *Selection*. Alas, my honoured Sir! a Selection is now out of my power. Many of thefe pieces, fince firft printed and publifhed, have been reprinted and republifhed without the privity or confent of the author; and ten to one, if the breath was out of his body, but fome other collection of this fort would be

PREFACE.

be offered to the Publick under his name, much lefs felect than the prefent; fwelled with articles, of which in the firft inftance he was not the retailer or manufacturer, and for which he ought not, dead or alive, to be made or thought refponfible.

Of the Contents of thefe Mifcellanies a fhort Summary is given at the conclufion of each volume; yet it appears neceffary to fpeak more at large, in the ftyle of a *Catalogue Raifonnée*, of fome of the Particulars.

The firft volume confifts entirely of Effays; a ftyle of writing to which the Author has always betrayed a great propenfity. This inclination led him, at a very early period, to offer the paper that opens the volume to the conductors of THE ADVENTURER, who honoured it with acceptance and infertion, fome time before the diftinguifhed æra when the illuftrious Mr. Town introduced himfelf to the notice

notice of the Publick under the title of THE CONNOISSEUR.

The Series of Papers, under the names of THE GENIUS and THE GENTLEMAN, were chiefly undertaken with a view of promoting the intereſt of the Publications in which they appeared, and with ſome thoughts of longer duration; but other avocations intervening, they were diſcontinued as abruptly as they were begun. For every thing in theſe papers the Editor is reſponſible, except for the *Epiſtle to a Friend* at the concluſion of No. XI. written by Mr. Lloyd.

The numbers of *TERRÆ-FILIUS* were written and publiſhed at the time of their ſeveral dates, during a party to Oxford in company with my old friends and ſchool-fellows Thornton and Churchill: neither of whom however took any part in that publication, though Thornton on our return frankly owned his regret at not having joined his old Co-adjutor.

The

PREFACE.

The second volume opens with a string of Letters and other articles, written for the same purpose as the main part of the Essays in the first; acting in concert with men whose names I loved, and whose memories I revere. A certain splenetick author, who confessedly dates the dawnings of his Genius from his juvenile effusions in a Weekly Journal, speaks in his usual style of Egotism with great contempt of the writers and sharers in News-Papers. For my part, not conscious of having written any thing in them for which I ought to be ashamed, I am free to confess my having written in them. Nor indeed ought *He* to blush at his earliest connections; but rather to pride himself, and assume more consequence than he now challenges, if possible, from the reflection of having conveyed his Loose Thoughts and Tritical Essays to the Publick through the same channel with the manly Lucubrations of Pulteney and Bolingbroke.

The

PREFACE.

The two Prefaces to the plays of Massinger and Beaumont and Fletcher, though conveying no Literary Doctrines which I do not avow, are not however to be strictly taken as coming from me as the Editor of either of those Publications, for which I do not consider myself as responsible. The Critical Reflections were thrown together at the instance of Mr. Garrick, to serve his old subject Davies; who, converted from an Actor into a Bookseller, had purchased the remaining copies of Coxeter's Edition of the Works of Massinger, to which he added the Critical Reflections as a Preface. Of the Edition of the Plays of Beaumont and Fletcher I never saw a line, to the best of my recollection, till near two volumes were printed. I afterwards revised the proof sheets, and by degrees interested myself still more in the publication; for which I had no other motive than the desire of preventing a probable loss to a person who had hazarded a very considerable sum on the undertaking.

PREFACE.

The Appendix to the second Edition of the Translation of Terence is inserted in these volumes, for the reasons assigned in the Postscript to that Appendix, now first published, to which Postscript I beg leave to refer the reader.

In this detail of the several parts of this Compilation, one of the first attempts at Verse that presents itself is an Ode to Oblivion and an Ode to Obscurity; in speaking of which I may say of this *Farrago*, as Othello of the story of his life,

"I ran it o'er ev'n from my boyish days."

These Odes were indeed a piece of boys' play with my schoolfellow Lloyd, with whom they were written in concert, in those days when we had so little grace as to ridicule our Poetical Masters, joking perhaps too licentiously with the *Prettynesses* of one poet, and the *Obscurities* of another. We were not however insensible to their real merits and excellencies, nor desirous to depreciate them: and if the time of the publication cannot
be

be admitted as an apology, it should be remembered that there are few writers who have not, in some part of their career, indulged themselves in similar liberties, and been guilty of the like transgressions. Repentance in these cases, as in most others, comes too late to redeem the offence. *Nescit vox missa reverti.* The Elegy of Isis, and the Poem of THE TRIUMPHS OF ISIS, are in vain excluded from the collections of their respective authors. They have been given to the world with the names of the writers, in other Miscellanies; and their native Spirit and Vigour has kept them alive, in spite of the efforts of their unnatural parents to stifle or overlay them.

THE LAW STUDENT has already been twice before the Publick, though not exactly in the same shape as at present; first in Lloyd's Poems, and afterwards in a collection entitled, *The Oxford Sausage,* entirely consisting of pieces written by Oxonians. Lloyd was removed to Cambridge, as I was to Oxford; yet

PREFACE.

yet I was concerned in the firſt of thoſe publications, and a ſtranger to the ſecond. The truth is that Lloyd wanted materials to fill a volume, undertaken by ſubſcription, and this little Poem contributed, with ſome variations, to ſupply the deficiency.

The next article will perhaps at firſt ſight ſtartle the reader, THE ROLLIAD, *an Heroick Poem!* Familiar, however, as the title may appear to his ear and eye, he may be aſſured that the preſent work had a being and a name long before the exiſtence of the popular and political work lately known under that title.

The reader I fear will ſoon diſcover that there is no other affinity or ſimilarity between the two poems. *What's in a name?* and even that name was given to the ſeveral works on different principles: for Commentators muſt agree, that the Political ROLLIAD derives its title, like the *Odyſſey*, the *Æneid*, and the *Henriade*, from the name of the
Hero;

Hero; while *our* ROLLIAD owes its denomination to the greatness of the event or the action, like the *Iliad*, the *Jerusalem*, and *Paradise Lost!*

The Cobbler of Cripplegate's Letter to R. Lloyd was written in concert with Garrick, and with Churchill's knowledge and privity sent to Lloyd for insertion in his monthly publication. Lloyd, on the receipt of it, consulted Churchill on the propriety of printing such an attack upon himself and his friends. In that point, says Churchill drily, you must judge for yourself. He did judge for himself, and published it: and considering the literary squabbles of that period, which this Letter tended to ridicule, I think he judged rightly.

This article reminds me of mentioning what I had nearly forgot; that the Epigram at the end of the Cock-Lane Ghost Intelligence was a *jeu d'esprit* of Garrick.

The

PREFACE.

The recapitulation of some of these circumstances will perhaps be less interesting to the reader than to the writer, whom they affect most sensibly, by recalling to his mind the memory of many pleasant hours never, never, to return!

> *O Noctes, Cœnæque Deûm!*
> ——*sollicit jucunda oblivia vitæ.*

The several articles in the second and third volumes, distinguished in the Summary of Contents by an asterisk, were written since the work was first committed to the press, and were indeed the chief amusements of the writer in the intervals of ease and leisure, during a severe and long illness. Two or three of them (but two or three, and those very short) have that illness for their subject; and the thirty-ninth Psalm comes so close to the original, which so naturally resolves itself into Blank Verse, that he is almost afraid of having misnamed it by styling it *an Imitation.*

These

These, and other additions, are now humbly offered to his readers, not without hopes of contributing to their entertainment. And indeed many parts of this collection have already been so favourably received, that the writer is unwilling to suppose, that by thus bringing together his detached pieces, he shall be considered as binding twigs to compose a rod for himself, while he is amused with the thoughts of making up a nosegay for his friends and for the Publick.

SUMMARY

SUMMARY OF THE CONTENTS.

VOL. I.

Page 1. THE ADVENTURER, No. XC. SACRIFICE BY THE AUTHORS OF THE EXCEPTIONABLE PARTS OF THEIR WORKS: A VISION. Ariſtotle and Longinus by Command of Apollo and the Muſes, Chief Prieſts; Horace, Quintilian, and Addiſon their principal Aſſiſtants. Offering of Homer returned by Longinus. Offering of Virgil, reſcued by two Romans. Offerings of other Greek and Roman Authors. Offerings of Chaucer and Dryden. Offering of Shakeſpeare, with the deciſions of Longinus and Ariſtotle on his writings and genius. Offerings of Milton, Beaumont and Fletcher, Otway, Rowe, and other Dramatick Writers, particularly of Sir John Vanbrugh. Pope's Sacrifice to Addiſon, with his return of the Offering and Anſwer. Irruption of the Freethinkers, who commit a large Volume to the flames. Triumph of the BIBLE, and defeat of the Freethinkers. Viſion concluded.

P. 11. THE GENIUS, No. I. CHARACTER OF A MODERN GENIUS. His progreſs through the Stages of Childhood, Youth, and Manhood. A Genius in

CONTENTS.

Life; A Genius in the Professions; and a Genius in Low Life, particularly as an Author.

Page 19. THE GENIUS, No. II. PORTRAIT OF THE AUTHOR, AND DESCRIPTION OF HIS PERSON. Inconveniencies and mortifications of being *remarkably low of stature*. Instances of GREAT AND WONDERFUL MEN OF THAT SIZE.

P. 31. THE GENIUS, No. III. LETTER FROM HUMPHRY GUBBINS, on the extravagance of his Wife in the article of Dress, particularly her expence in jewels.

Letter from a Sportsman to engage the GENIUS as a Jockey.

P. 43. THE GENIUS, No. IV. REFLECTIONS ON THE CONSEQUENCES OF THE PEACE. Its effects on Dress, on Travel, on Publick Places, and on Publick Prints. Idea of a PATRIOT KING cultivating the ARTS OF PEACE.

P. 52. THE GENIUS, No. V. PRESENT STATE OF A COUNTRY LIFE, owing to the easy intercourse between the most distant parts of the kingdom and the metropolis. Hints to the Country Gentlemen.

P. 60. THE GENIUS, No. VI. ON SLANDER. Modern improvements in that elegant and refined art. Characters of Lady JACYNTHA SCANDAL and JACKY TATTLE.

Page 69.

CONTENTS.

Page 69. THE GENIUS, No. VII. ON THE ROYAL WEDDING AND CORONATION. Letter from *Thaleſtris Dymock*, the Championeſs. Ode to a Weather-cock.

P. 78. THE GENIUS, No. VIII. ACCOUNT OF THE READING DESK OF THE GENIUS IN THE BRITISH MUSEUM. Extracts from a curious Manuſcript Hiſtory of the Iſland of ANEMOLIA, written by Petrus Ægidius, of Antwerp, to whom Sir Thomas More inſcribed his Hiſtory of UTOPIA. Of the Language and Literature of the ANEMOLIANS. Of their love of *Liberty* and *Property*.

P. 86. THE GENIUS, No. IX. LETTER FROM PATIENCE GREENFIELD, the Lady of a Member of Parliament who has greatly injured his fortune by *being brought in for nothing*, and is likely to compleat his ruin by the misfortune of having carried his election.

P. 96. THE GENIUS, No. X. LETTER FROM JOHN TROT; ſhort reflections on it, followed by further extracts from the Hiſtory of ANEMOLIA. Of the *Anemolian Women*, their uncommon beauty, and the means they uſe to deſtroy it. Of their dreſs, imported from *Achoria*. Of licenced Courtezans, Drunkards, Swearers, and Gameſters. Of ſuits at law. Of the Anemolian Religion, Sects of Deiſts, Polytheiſts, and Atheiſts, ſome few Profeſſors of Chriſtianity. The ANEMOLIANS *conſtitutional ſuicides*. Page 108.

CONTENTS.

Page 108. THE GENIUS, No. XI. ON THE FREQUENT AND VIOLENT QUARRELS AMONG AUTHORS, their abfurdity and ill confequences. *A Poetical Epiſtle to a Friend.*

P. 117. THE GENIUS, No. XII. ON GOOD HUMOUR, One of the firſt requifites in Society. *Conſtitutional Good Humour.* The Engliſh in general rather *good natured* than *good-humoured.* Good Humour often gradually loſt in the progreſs of life. Character of an Ill-Humoured Man. Good-Humour one of the moſt captivating qualities in a *Woman.* Good-Humour particularly recommended *to Authors.*

P. 126. THE GENIUS, No. XIII. A Converfation on the ſtrange diverſities of temper and underſtanding among mankind. VISION arifing from it; in which the Genius of the Elements accounts to the Dreamer for the various difpoſitions of his fellow-creatures.

P. 136. THE GENIUS, No. XIV. ON THE WATERING PLACES. Reflections on a Trip to Bath. What is the chief difference between Bath and London. Invalids not the greater part of the company. Of Gaming, Courtſhip, and Intrigue. On female *fortune-hunters*, and male and female *toad-eaters.* Propofals for a fubfcription towards the publication or fuppreffion of *The Secret Hiſtory of Bath and Tunbridge.*

P. 147. THE GENIUS, No. XV. A CARD FROM MRS. MARCOURT. Her character. Defcription of her

private

CONTENTS.

private Party. *Routes* defcribed and refined. Reflections on thofe Affemblies. Heads of a bill to prevent their further ill confequences. Plan of the ROUT-ACT.

Page 161. THE GENTLEMAN, No. I. The PUBLICK SPIRIT OF AUTHORS. Their quiet furrender of the PROPERTY *of the Prefs.* Their conftant zeal for the LIBERTY *of the Prefs.* Intentions of the GENTLEMAN. Comments on his motto. Reafons for the name he has affumed, and motives of the prefent publication.

P. 169. THE GENTLEMAN, No. II. Letters from two Correfpondents: the firft from a BLACKGUARD, reprobating the modern fyftem of *Gentility*; the fecond from a fair INCOGNITA, offering her advice and affiftance in all *female cafes.*

P. 178. THE GENTLEMAN, No. III. ON the prefent STATE OF LEARNING. ON PURITY OF STYLE. On the imitation of Living Authors, and neglect of the works of Deceafed Writers. Of falfe Ornaments. Of *Idiom.* Proper ufe of Grammars and Dictionaries.

P. 187. THE GENTLEMAN, No. IV. A fecond Letter from- The BLACKGUARD. ON THE STYLE OF CONVERSATION. Bye words and cant terms, calculated to damp and deftroy all pleafantry and improvement. Remonftrance againft the ufe of the words *Patch* and *Bore.*

Page 196.

CONTENTS.

Page 196. THE GENTLEMAN, No. V. HISTORY OF A VISIT TO SIR JOCELYN HEARTY, DURING THE SUMMER RECESS. His domeſtick employments. His politicks. A meeting of the Juſtices. A Turnpike meeting. The Races. The Aſſizes. The Grand Jury. The *Conſtitution* and Eſtate neceſſary to ſupport the Character of a *Country Gentleman*.

P. 204. THE GENTLEMAN, No. VI. A third Letter from THE BLACKGUARD. On DRAMATICK CRITICISM. The inviduous compariſon of Moderns with Ancients, and Moderns with Moderns. On *reigning words*, LOW, SENTIMENT, &c. uſed as weapons of Criticiſm. *Nature* the only word that ſhould have currency or authority. *Manneriſts* in Criticiſm or Compoſition equally reprehenſible.

P. 215. Prefatory Letter to the Eſſays of TERRÆ-FILIUS.

P. 217. TERRÆ-FILIUS, No. I. Notice of the arrival of TERRÆ-FILIUS. Conſequences of his advertiſements announcing himſelf, in the London and Oxford papers. His Rights and Privileges aſſerted. His Character as eſſential to the ENCÆNIA, as that of the Publick Orator. Denunciations of puniſhment againſt delinquents; but trial and ſentence of criminals poſtponed till to-morrow.

Advertiſement of new publications.

P. 230. TERRÆ-FILIUS, No. II. SCANDAL THE MOST PROFITABLE COMMODITY FOR A DEALER IN LITERATURE.

CONTENTS.

LITERATURE. / Shop opened during the ENCÆNIA by TERRÆ-FILIUS. *Who is* TERRÆ-FILIUS? Various conjectures referred to time for a discovery. POSTSCRIPT containing an extract from the University Statutes, with a translation.

P. 242. TERRÆ-FILIUS, No. III. REFLECTIONS ON THE REIGNING PASSION FOR SHEWS AND FESTIVALS. Particular account of a Trip to Oxford during the ENCÆNIA, by Mr. and Mrs. Folio, on a visit to Young Folio. Their remarks on the University, its buildings, its studies, &c.

P. 254. TERRÆ-FILIUS, No. IV. THE HARANGUE OF TERRÆ-FILIUS ON LAYING DOWN HIS OFFICE. Vindication of his character, and the manner in which he has discharged his duty. POSTSCRIPT, with clauses from the Penal Statutes of the University.

PROSE
ON SEVERAL OCCASIONS.

THE ADVENTURER: N° 90.

Saturday, September 15th, 1753.

Concretam exemit labem, purumque reliquit
Ætherium sensum, atque auraï simplicis ignem. VIRGIL.

No speck is left of their habitual stains,
But the pure æther of the soul remains. DRYDEN.

NOTHING sooner quells the ridiculous triumph of human vanity, than reading those passages of the greatest writers in which they seem deprived of that noble spirit that inspires them in other parts; and where, instead of invention and grandeur, we meet with nothing but flatness and insipidity.

The pain I have felt in observing a lofty genius thus sink beneath itself, has often made me wish that thefe unworthy ftains could be blotted from their works, and leave them perfect and immaculate.

I went to bed a few nights ago full of thefe thoughts, and clofed the evening, as I frequently do, with reading a few lines of Virgil. I accidentally opened that part of the fixth book; where Anchifes recounts to his fon the various methods of purgation which the foul undergoes in the next world, to cleanfe it from the filth it has contracted by its connections with the body, and to deliver the pure ætherial effence from the vicious tincture of mortality. This was fo much like my evening's fpeculation, that it infenfibly mixed and incorporated with it, and as foon as I fell afleep formed itfelf into the following dream.

I found myfelf in an inftant in the midft of a temple, which was built with all that magnificent fimplicity, that diftinguifhes the productions of the ancients. At the Eaft end was raifed an altar, on each fide of which ftood a prieft who feemed preparing to facrifice. On the altar was kindled a fire, from which arofe the brighteft flame I had ever beheld. The light which it difpenfed, though remarkably ftrong and clear, was not quivering and dazzling, but fteady and uniform, and diffufed a purple radiance through the whole edifice, not unlike the firft appearance of the morning.

While

While I stood fixed in admiration, my attention was awakened by the blast of a trumpet that shook the whole temple; but it carried a certain sweetness in its sound, which mellowed and tempered the natural shrillness of that instrument. After it had sounded thrice, the Being who blew it, habited according to the description of Fame by the ancients, issued a proclamation to the following purpose. " By command of Apollo and the Mu-
" ses, all who have ever made any pretensions to
" fame by their writings are enjoined to sacrifice
" upon the altar in this temple those parts of their
" works, which have hitherto been preserved to
" their infamy; that their names may descend
" spotless and unsullied to posterity. For this
" purpose Aristotle and Longinus are appointed
" chief priests, who are to see that no improper
" oblations are made, and no proper ones con-
" cealed; and, for the more easy performance of
" this office, they are allowed to chuse as their
" assistants whomsoever they shall think worthy of
" the function."

As soon as this proclamation was made I turned my eyes with inexpressible delight towards the two priests; but was soon robbed of the pleasure of looking at them by a croud of people running

running up to offer their service. These I found to be a groupe of French criticks; but their offers were rejected by both priests with the utmost indignation, and their whole works were thrown on the altar, and reduced to ashes in an instant. The two priests then looked round, and chose with a few others Horace and Quintilian from among the Romans, and Addison from the English, as their principal assistants.

The first who came forward with his offering, by the loftiness of his demeanor was soon discovered to be Homer. He approached the altar with great majesty, and delivered to Longinus those parts of his Odyssey, which have been censured as improbable fictions, and the ridiculous narratives of old age. Longinus was preparing for the sacrifice; but observing that Aristotle did not seem willing to assist him in the office, he returned them to the venerable old bard with great deference, saying that " they were indeed the tales of old age, but it " was the old age of Homer."

Virgil appeared next, and approached the altar with a modest dignity in his gait and countenance peculiar to himself, and to the surprise of all committed his whole Æneid to the flames. But it was immediately rescued by two Romans, who ran

with

with precipitation to the altar, delivered the poem from deftruction, and carried off the author between them, repeating that glorious boaft of about forty lines at the beginning of the third Georgick.

———Tentanda via eft ; quâ me quoque poffim
Tollere humo, victorque virûm volitare per ora.
Primus ego in patriam mecum &c.

After him moft of the Greek and Roman authors proceeded to the altar, and furrendered with great modefty and humility the moft faulty part of their works. One circumftance was obfervable; that the facrifice always increafed, in proportion as the author had ventured to deviate from a judicious imitation of Homer. The latter Roman authors, who feemed almoft to have loft fight of him, made fo large offerings, that fome of their works, which were before very voluminous, fhrunk into the compafs of a primer.

It gave me the higheft fatisfaction to fee philofophy thus cleared from erroneous principles, hiftory purged of falfehood, poetry of fuftian, and nothing left in each but genius, fenfe and truth. I marked with particular attention the feveral offerings of the moft eminent Englifh writers. Chaucer gave up his obfcenity, and then delivered
his

his works to Dryden to clear them from the rubbish that encumbered them. Dryden executed his task with great address, and, as Addison says of Virgil in his Georgicks, " tossed about his dung with " an air of gracefulness." He not only repaired the injuries of time, but threw in a thousand new graces. He then advanced towards the altar himself, and delivered up a large paquet which contained many plays, and some poems. The paquet had a label affixed to it which bore this inscription, " To Poverty."

Shakespeare carried to the altar a long string of puns marked " The taste of the age," a small parcel of bombast, and a pretty large bundle of incorrectness. Notwithstanding the ingenuous air with which he made this offering, some officiates at the altar accused him of concealing certain pieces, and mentioned the London Prodigal, Sir Thomas Cromwell, the Yorkshire Tragedy, &c. The poet replied, that " as those pieces were unworthy to be " preserved, he should see them consumed to ashes " with great pleasure, but that he was wholly in-" nocent of their original." The two chief priests interposed in this dispute, and dismissed the poet with many compliments; Longinus observing that the pieces in question could not possibly be his, for
that

that the failings of Shakespeare were like those of Homer, " whose genius, whenever it subsided, " might be compared to the ebbing of the ocean, " which left a mark upon its shores to shew to " what a height it was sometimes carried." Aristotle concurred in this opinion, and added " that although Shakespeare was quite ignorant of " that exact œconomy of the stage, which is so " remarkable in the Greek writers, yet the meer " strength of his genius had in many points car- " ried him infinitely beyond them."

Milton gave up a few errors in his Paradise Lost, and the sacrifice was attended with great decency by Addison. Otway and Rowe threw their comedies upon the altar, and Beaumont and Fletcher the two last acts of many of their pieces. They were followed by Tom Durfey, Etherege, Wycherley, and several other dramatic writers, who made such large contributions that they set the altar in a blaze.

Among these I was surprized to see an author, with much politeness in his behaviour and spirit in his countenance, tottering under an unwieldy burden. As he approached I discovered him to be Sir John Vanbrugh, and could not but smile, when on his committing his heavy load to the flames, it proved to be " his skill in architecture."

Pope advanced towards Addison, and delivered with great humility those lines written expressly against him, so remarkable for their excellence and their cruelty, repeating this couplet;

> " Curst be the verse, how well soe'er it flow
> " That tends to make one worthy man my foe."

The ingenious critick insisted on his taking them again, " for" said he " my associates at the altar, " particularly Horace, would never permit a line " of so excellent a satirist to be consumed. The " many compliments paid me in other parts of " your works amply compensate for this slight in- " dignity; and be assured, that no little pique or " misunderstanding shall ever make me a foe to " genius." Pope bowed in some confusion, and promised to substitute a fictitious name at least, which was all that was left in his power. He then retired, after having made a sacrifice of a little paquet of Antitheses, and some parts of his translation of Homer.

During the course of these oblations, I was charmed with the candour, decency, and judgment, with which all the priests discharged their different functions. They behaved with such dignity that it reminded

reminded me of those ages, when the offices of king and priest centered in the same person. Whenever any of the assistants were at a loss in any particular circumstances, they applied to Aristotle, who settled the whole business in an instant.

But the reflections, which this pleasing scene produced, were soon interrupted by a tumultuous noise at the gate of the temple; when suddenly a rude illiterate multitude rushed in, led by Tindal, Morgan, Chubb and Bolingbroke. The chiefs, whose countenances were impressed with rage whch art could not conceal, forced their way to the altar, and amidst the joyful acclamations of their followers threw a large volume into the fire. But the triumph was short, and joy and acclamation gave way to silence and astonishment. The Volume lay unhurt in the midst of the fire, and, as the flames played innocently about it, I could discover, written in letters of gold, the words THE BIBLE. At that instant my ears were ravished with the sound of more than mortal musick, accompanying a hymn, sung by invisible beings, of which I well remember the following verses:

" The words of the Lord are pure words: even
" as the silver, which in the earth is tried, and
" purified seven times in the fire.
                                    " More

"More to be defired are they than gold; yea, than much fine gold; fweeter alfo than honey, and the honey-comb."

The united melody of inftruments and voices, which formed a concert fo exquifite, that as Milton fays " it might create a foul under the ribs " of death," threw me into fuch extafies, that I was awakened by their violence.

THE GENIUS.
NUMBER I.

Lemmata si quæris cur sint adscripta, docebo:
Ut, si malueris, Lemmata sola legas. MART.

Mottoes! why Mottoes, Sir? you cry:
I'll tell you, Sir, the reason why.
'Tis that, dull prose dull prose succeeding,
You may at least find verse worth reading.

A GENIUS is a character purely modern, and of so late an origin, that it has never yet been described or defined in any treatise, essay, lexicon, or dictionary. It is now, however, become almost universal. The originals are, indeed, so numerous, and the features so strong, that it requires but little skill to take an exact likeness. I am myself an acknowledged GENIUS; and since it is no more than drawing my own picture, I cannot better introduce myself to the reader, than by giving at one stroke a rough draught of my own character, and that of the numerous fraternity, by way of preliminary paper, or frontispiece, if you please, to the ensuing speculations.

The

The ancients, according to their wonted narrowness of soul, honoured a very small portion of the human race with this appellation. He, who to extraordinary talents had added extraordinary application, after the most arduous efforts towards excellence in some one art or science, was perhaps at last fortunate enough to extort this distinction. The more generous moderns demand only the first requisites; and even those, like the places of men ballotted into the militia, may be supplied by substitutes. Vanity or assurance may pass, in the modern muster, for superior faculties. The GENIUS, endowed with them, needs neither diligence nor assiduity. Supported by confidence, he disdains to halt along on the crutches of application. So far from being versed merely in one science, he runs round the whole circle at his pleasure. Knowledge is rained down on his head like manna from heaven, and he has no care but to gather it as it falls. Almost every man is an adept in every art; acquires learning without study; improves his good sense without meditation; writes without reading; and, being full as well acquainted with one thing as another, is an unquestionable GENIUS; or, what is more extraordinary, maintains his right to that title without knowing, or even pretending to know, any thing at all.

There

There is a certain reverend and affecting biographer in this town, who pens, almost every six weeks, the memoirs of several unfortunate great men, and among them of many a GENIUS. In order to shew the characters of his heroes at full length, he takes up their adventures, *e'en from their boyish days*, and fairly sets down a plain account of their life, character, and behaviour, beginning with their birth, parentage, and education; so that the reader may see at one glance, by what steps they have gained the top-most round of the ladder. In imitation of so great an example, I will endeavour to trace the GENIUS almost from his birth to his sublimest stage of excellence. GENIUS is, indeed, universally allowed to be the gift of nature : we cannot therefore be surprised to find it, like Hercules, exerting its strength in the cradle.

The cradle, indeed, may be considered as a mere hot-bed for the raising of GENIUS; which is a plant of so delicate a nature, that it is often nipt in the bud. There never was a child, as its parents will tell you, who did not soon give evident tokens of the brightest parts, by doing and saying ten thousand witty things, which were never done or said before since the infancy of Cain and Abel.

The wit of a child, like that of a monkey, (which is a very wife animal, and, we are told, could speak if it would) confifts in mifchief; and the more fpirit little mafter poffeffes, the more entertaining he is to the company. I remember, that I was once taken fo much notice of for my wit and humour in pulling off a grave gentleman's wig, that it afterwards betrayed me into feveral fcrapes, by playing the fame tricks over again upon dull fellows, who had not fuch ftrong ideas of pleafantry. It may not be amifs to obferve here, that practical ftrokes of humour are thofe, in which a GENIUS takes the moft delight.

At fchool the young GENIUS will begin to heighten our expectations of his future abilities. His parts, indeed, will be too brilliant to attend the inftructions he might receive there; but his fpirit will have more room to difplay itfelf. He may be at the bottom of his clafs, but he will be at the head of every fcrape. He may be deficient in Greek and Latin, make falfe concord in his profe, and be guilty of falfe quantities in his verfe; yet, before he leaves fchool, he will not be unacquainted with the world, will walk familiarly into a tavern, know the beft fongs at Comus's court, and the names and perfons of the kindeft ladies upon town. But, when

when once relieved from scholastick restraints, as his sphere will be more noble, his fame will become more eminent. If he is entered at either of our universities, the tameness of an academical life being ill adapted to the vivacity of his disposition, he will spend all his time in Covent Garden by way of being in genteel company. If he is sent abroad, because, forsooth, his wise parents or guardians imagine that the discipline of our own universities is not strict enough, he will soon convince them that the government of foreign academies is infinitely more lax. He will speedily distinguish himself by his uncommon spirit; and after shooting a waiter, killing his friend in a duel, or perhaps contaminating the sixty descents in the house of a German baron by decoying his daughter, he may ride post out of the continent, and be glad to embark in a storm in order to get safe footing in Old England.

Old England is, indeed, the noblest theatre in the universe for a GENIUS. Here he may go through all the changes and diversities of his character at pleasure. Here he may send his mistress to parade through the streets in a gilt chariot, drawn by pyebald horses; he may at the same time be so deeply engaged at play, that his own chariot may

stand

stand at the door of Arthur's till eight in the morning. He may ride his own matches at Newmarket, and perform new miracles againſt time and weight, and number of horſes, every ſeaſon. In a word, he may indulge his vivacity in every ebullition of GENIUS, from toſſing off his quarts of champagne, to ſhooting himſelf through the head.

With this ſpirit and vivacity may a GENIUS of quality and eſtate employ himſelf: but as talents are the gift of nature, and riches the mere favours of fortune, it happens unluckily, that many a GENIUS is reduced to the mean reſources of trade or profeſſion to ſupport himſelf. In theſe caſes, if the warmth of a GENIUS is not abated, it involves him in many difficulties. The ſpirit of the clerk in a compting-houſe may perhaps betray him into a forgery; and the evil GENIUS of the apprentice may tempt him to commit depredations on the till.

The young phyſician of GENIUS, inſtead of throwing that ſolemnity into his countenance, which would make him look as if he had himſelf taken the potion he ſhould preſcribe, adopts a whimſical air, and ſoon loſes his credit with the old practitioners, the apothecaries, and his brother-attendants at the hoſpital, by laughing at the farce of phyſick, and ſwearing that water-gruel is

of

of infinitely more fervice than the whole Materia Medica. A GENIUS of this fpecies fometimes retrieves himfelf by recurring irregularly to phyfick, and hawking a *noftrum*.

The lively ftudent at the inns of court has too fublime a turn of mind to follow his profeffion. He gives the attornies a contempt for him by endeavouring to converfe with them facetioufly; and is feen walking the ftreets in an illegal bag-wig, inftead of prudently wearing the bufinefs-following bob. He may be found oftener behind the fcenes at the play-houfe, than in the courts of juftice; and if he is a prodigious GENIUS indeed, he even writes for the ftage.

The exploits of a modern GENIUS in high life are indeed no where to be equalled, except by the productions of a modern GENIUS in low life, as an author. His works are not to be eftimated according to the quality, but the quantity of them; and they are fold, wholefale and retail, to one fet of bookfellers, as another fet of bookfellers in Moorfields fell thofe of his predeceffors—by the pound. He is not only capable of writing in any fcience, but he will undertake to write in all fciences at once. He will publifh in one day detached parcels of biography, architecture, hufbandry, husbandry, gardening, and cookery. He will be, at one and the same time, the author of a long history, the translator of a voluminous foreign writer, the inventor of a novel, the conductor of a review, the Doer of a magazine, and the manager of a news-paper. In comparison to him, Tully shall appear to have written a volume no bigger than the primer, and the Iliad shall shrink into a nutshell. Longinus, from his great learning, was denominated a walking musæum; and our GENIUS, from the number and quality of his productions, may be more familiarly stiled a circulating library.

Such an author am I, the GENIUS. History shall stand still for events, and I will transcribe the news-papers, as the annals of politicks and literature, 'ere my pen shall cease to go on. Loose papers, such as these, will scarce engage the attention of a moment, and will be hastily scribbled over at the tea-table, just when the whim shall sieze me, or any amusing thoughts come uppermost in the whirl of my imagination. The reader therefore must not expect me at certain periods, since I shall always pop abruptly in upon him. Sometimes he may see me once, sometimes twice, in a week; and sometimes perhaps not above once in a fortnight

fortnight. I hope to wait on him again very soon; and, as I have here faid fomething of my difpofition and fituation, I propofe in my next to give an exact defcription of my perfon.

THE GENIUS.
NUMBER II.

Τυδευς, μικρον δεμας, αλλα μαχητης.   HOMER.

TYDEUS, of perfon fmall! what then?
Great heroes may be little men.

NOTWITHSTANDING the eminent advantages refulting from the many rare talents and qualities neceffarily included in that illuftrious character defcribed in my firft paper, under the title of a GENIUS, I am, I muft confefs, neither the moft completely happy, nor moft univerfally accomplifhed man in the creation. Nature, who has in fome inftances been lavifh in her bounties to me, has in others been rather too unkind, and indeed remarkably niggard of her favours. Vanity, for example, fhe has fo exuberantly poured upon me, that my portion, to fay no more of it, is at leaft fufficient to embolden me to venture forth as an author; and yet my fenfibility is, at the fame time, unfortunately fo nice and exquifite, that it

becomes

becomes a perpetual thorn in the sides of that very vanity, laying it open to every slight attack, and rendering it too easily wounded by the petulance of folly, the slanders of envy, the gross jests of buffoonery, or the malice of a review.

But the greatest drawback, which nature has, in my case, made on that vanity and self-applause, which contributes more or less to the happiness of every man and woman in the world, is most unfortunately external; visible to all eyes, open to general observation, and liable to ridicule from the dullest fellow, that casts a look upon my person. Peculiarities of figure, whether in make, size, or complexion, have always been deemed an inexhaustible source of ridicule to the associates of the man who possesses them. He, whose person is remarkable, seems to be considered as a butt, planted by nature, for all other men to shoot their wit at. The coarse humour of our own vulgar, however blind to mental blemishes, is sharp-sighted as a lynx to external defects, and exerts itself as liberally on genteeler passers-by, as on their own hump-backed companion, whom they jocularly entitle, *my lord*. Homer represents the gods themselves as laughing at the ugly, awkward, blacksmith divinity of Vulcan. Tully in his Dialogues *de Oratore*,

recommends

recommends it to an orator to be pleasant and facetious on personal defects; though perhaps rather unadvisedly, and unsuitably to the grave dignity of that profession: and, now we are got so deep in learned quotations, I defy the scholar to find in Lucian, Aristophanes, Theophrastus, or any other author, ancient or modern, a greater profusion of wit and humour bestowed on any one subject, than Shakespeare has lavished, in his several descriptions of Falstaff, Shallow, and Bardolph, on a fat man, a lean man, and a man with a red nose. Happy indeed would it be for any other man, (especially if he be a wit and a GENIUS) who bears about in his person this native fund of pleasantry: if he could say with Falstaff, and with equal justice too, "I am not only witty myself, but also the cause of wit in other men."

Let not, however, the partial reader conclude too hastily from what has been said, that I pretend to the honour of the deformity of Scarron, the crookedness of Pope, the blindness of Milton or Homer, or even the long nose, or no nose of Tristram Shandy. Not to make any further delay of introduction, after having so long announced myself to the good company, the truth, and the whole truth, is, that I am of a remarkable low stature;

stature; a sort of diminutive plaything of Madam Nature, that seems to have been made, like a girl's doll, to divert the good lady in her infancy; a little *i* without a tittle o'top; an human figure in miniature; a make-weight in the scale of mortality; a minim of nature; a mannikin, not to say minnikin; and indeed rather an abstract or brief chronicle of man's fair proportions, than a man at large. My person, indeed, is not formed in that excellent mould of littleness, which, as in some insects and animals, becomes beautiful from the nice texture and curious composition of its parts. I may be seen, it is true, without the help of a microscope; and am not even qualified to rival the dwarf *Coan*, by being exhibited to my worthy countrymen at six-pence a-piece. I am, however, so low in stature, that my name is hardly ever mentioned without the epithet *little* being prefixed to it: the moment that my person presents itself among strange company, the first idea that strikes the beholders is the minuteness of the figure, and a whisper instantly buzzes round the room, *lord! what a little creature!* As I walk along the street, I hear the men and women say to one another, *there goes a little man!* — In a word, it is my irreparable misfortune to be, without

out my shoes, little more than five feet in height. Eating of daisy-roots, we are told, will retard a man's growth: if the French alimentary powder, or any other new-invented diet, would at once *elevate* me, and *surprise* my friends, I would go through a long regimen to be raised ever so little nearer heaven. I think I could not endure to have my limbs stretched to a nobler length in the bed of Procrustes; but, if I could be rolled out like dough or paste, or extended by relaxation, like a rope or an eel's skin in dry weather, I believe I should readily assent to it: for there is no impossibility existing in nature, or recorded in scripture, at the truth of which I am more apt to repine, than that *no man is able to add a cubit to his stature.*

When the camel applied to heaven for some amendment in his figure, Jupiter (says the fabulist) cropt his ears for his impertinence. I should be very loth, like some of my cotemporaries of the quill, by any means to endanger my ears; and yet nothing but the back of the camel being placed on my little body, could make me wish more ardently, than I do at present, for an happy alteration in it. For not to mention the natural inconveniencies of being trampled on and run over in a croud, almost prest to death by huge fellows and fat old women in machines and stage-coaches, deprived of all pleasure at sights and shews by taller persons taking their places before me;—not to dwell, I say, on these and several other circumstances of the same nature, it provokes me to find, that though I can sometimes as absolutely forget my littleness, as if I was as big as Goliah, yet my friends and acquaintance cannot, for one moment, lose the consideration of it. The minuteness of my person so entirely governs their idea of my character, that they are not able to detach the contemplation of one from the other; and from the mere credit of having a larger quantity of clay and dirt put together in their huge frames than myself, they become (as Beatrice terms it) such *valiant pieces of dust*, that a man who has room enough in his bosom for more gall than a pigeon, must be moved with indignation. If they think of my marriage, they set themselves to consider, what fairy they shall find for me, or whether it would not be better to cross the breed by providing me an amazon: they would have my chariot, like queen Mab's, made out of an hazel-nut: and as to an house, *the case of a treble hautboy were a mansion for me.*

A very

A very intimate friend of mine one day inadvertently betrayed to me, that his wife always spoke of me by the name of *the baby*; but afterwards, in order to mend the matter, he added, that she had no contemptible opinion of my person, for that she always said, " she never saw *such a little man* that was so *strait*." In families, where I visit, growing lads of thirteen or fourteen years of age are called out to stand back to back with me, and measure whether there is any difference between their height and mine: and once, I remember, on my visit to an acquaintance newly-married, being introduced to the bride, who was a fine tall woman, (but a prude or a wit, I cannot tell which) she held her head so high, without making the least inclination of her body, that I could as easily have scaled the monument, as have come at the tip of her chin without the help of a pair of steps. One day, just after the passing of the broad-wheel act, being on the road on a little poney, the man of the turnpike seeing me and my nag approach, cried out, " Nay, nay, this must " be above weight, I am sure." and, closing the gate, left me to go over the place appointed for weighing the waggons. Another time, after having dined at a nobleman's house, I was honoured

with

with the use of his lordship's chariot to carry me home, but was desired first to set down another of the company at St. James's coffee-house. My fellow traveller, if I may so call him, was one of the biggest and tallest men in the kingdom, and was at least four and twenty stone in weight. Thus ridiculously coupled, like a lean rabbit and a fat one, we engaged the attention of the whole street, particularly of the company at Arthur's, who stood laughing, as we passed by, to see the body of the chariot inclined all one way, as if we were driving on the slope of a hill, though the wheels ran on as smoothly and evenly as Madam Catharina's clockwork equipage on a parlour floor. But I must declare, that the most ridiculous distress I ever underwent, was, when my unfortunate curiosity carried me to see that wonderful phænomenon of nature, the Italian Giant, scarce less than eight feet high! While the rest of the company were walking under his arm, he seemed to expect that I should have crept between his legs; and, when I offered to present him with the usual gratuity, he absolutely refused to accept it, saying, " that he thought it full as great a curiosity to see me, as I could possibly think it to see him."—In short, my situation is almost as ridiculous as

that

that of Gulliver in Brobdignag; and though I cannot, like him, be carried to the ridge of a housetop by a monkey, or be stuck upright by an unlucky lad in a marrowbone, yet every day brings with it fresh instances of mortification.

But there is no circumstance moves my spleen more forcibly than the insolence of those, whose stature very little exceeds my own, and who seem to look down on such urchins as myself with a consciousness of their happy superiority. One of these always affects to call me *the little man*; and another small gentleman (a great actor I mean, whom in some future *histrio-mastix*, some *nescio quid majus* ROSCIADE, I may possibly take a peg or two lower) is fond of sidling up to me in all publick places, as second-rate beauties commonly contrive to take a dowdy abroad with them for a foil. For my own part, though I could wish to be taller, I never made use of any undue arts to appear so. I am content to submit my littleness, fairly to the world. I never suffered my hat to rise into the air with a staring *Kevenhuller*, and I would as soon appear in stilts, as be lifted from the ground by double soles or high heels to my shoes. I rather endeavour to console myself by looking abroad into the world for great men of another order than those

those described by serjeant Kite: and so successful have been my researches of this kind, that I could set down a long catalogue of persons eminent in the state, in the professions, in arts and sciences, (not to mention authors and actors) who are scarce taller than myself;. so that in this respect, we may fairly pronounce in favour of the present period, as Lord Clarendon has declared of his own, that " it was an age in which there were many GREAT and WONDERFUL MEN OF THAT SIZE." I do not know whether in this extremity of war, any new raised regiment offers bounty-money for volunteers five feet high ; but we flatter ourselves that, in case an invasion should take place, we could form a corps infinitely more formidable than the late king of Prussia's useless tall regiment.

I cannot close this paper without returning my thanks to the learned university of Oxford, and to the illustrious Queensbury family, for having published the above-mentioned papers of Lord Clarendon, in which there is much matter of consolation to gentlemen of the like height and dimensions with myself. It there appears, that most of his lordship's intimate friends were *great* and *wonderful men* of *low stature*. Mr. Hales, he tells us, was one of the least men in the kingdom, and one

of

of the greateſt ſcholars in Europe. Mr. Chillingworth was of a ſtature little ſuperior to Mr. Hales. Of his friend Sidney Godolphin he ſays, that there never was ſo great a mind and ſpirit contained in ſo little room; ſo large an underſtanding, and ſo unreſtrained a fancy, in ſo very ſmall a body. Of Sir Lucius Carey, afterwards lord Falkland, who was but little taller than Sidney Godolphin, he ſpeaks ſo highly, that I cannot reſiſt the temptation of gratifying myſelf and all other little men by tranſcribing the deſcription of his perſon, hoping it may ſerve to recommend us to the favour of the world, and particularly to the good graces of the ladies, who are deſired to take notice, that Sir Lucius married for love, and made a moſt excellent huſband. Lord Clarendon ſpeaks thus of him—" with theſe advantages he had one great diſadvantage (which in the firſt entrance into the world is attended with too much prejudice) in his perſon and preſence, which was in no degree attractive or promiſing. His ſtature was low, and ſmaller than moſt men; his motion not graceful; and his aſpect ſo far from inviting, that it had ſomewhat in it of ſimplicity: and his voice the worſt of the three, and ſo untuned, that inſtead of reconciling, it offended the ears, that no body would

would have expected mufick from that tongue. And fure no man was lefs beholden to nature for it's recommendation into the world: but then no man fooner, or more, difappointed this general and cuftomary prejudice. That little perfon and fmall ftature was quickly found to contain a great heart, a courage fo keen, and a nature fo fearlefs, that no compofition of the ftrongeft limbs, and moft harmonious and proportioned prefence and ftrength, ever more difpofed any man to the greateft enterprife; it being his greateft weaknefs to be too folicitous for fuch adventures: and that untuned tongue and voice, eafily difcovered itfelf to be fupplied, and governed, by a mind and underftanding fo excellent, that the wit and weight of all he faid, carried another kind of luftre, and admiration in it, and even another kind of acceptation from the perfons prefent, than any ornament of delivery could reafonably promife itfelf, or is ufually attended with; and his difpofition and nature was fo gentle and obliging, fo much delighted in courtefy, kindnefs, and generofity, that all mankind could not but admire and love him."

After this extract from Lord Chancellor Clarendon, I beg leave to addrefs myfelf to all little men, who are defirous to become great and wonderful,
like

like Sir Lucius, intreating them to meditate attentively for that end on the following maxim of that other great chancellor, Lord Bacon; which maxim may also serve as a sort of moral to this long paper on a short man : *whosoever hath any thing fixt in his person that doth induce contempt, hath also a perpetual spur in himself to rescue and deliver himself from scorn.*

THE GENIUS.
NUMBER III.

*Sardonychas, smaragdos, adamantas, iaspidas, uno
Versat in articulo Stella.*   MART.

Stella's bespankled o'er at every point:
Diamonds, pearls, rubies, on each single joint.

AFTER having kept the discourse entirely to myself, and made myself the delightful subject of that discourse for two whole papers, I am glad of an opportunity to relieve my readers by publishing the two following letters.

To the GENIUS.

SIR,   *Crutched friars, June 15, 1761.*

I AM a plain man, but I can see how this world goes for all that; and, indeed, to find out where the shoe pinches, requires no very fine feelings in him that wears it. My grievance is no small one I assure you. Give me leave, therefore, to submit my case to you and the publick; a case which affects not myself alone, but, more or less, many thousands also of honest peaceable married men in his majesty's dominions.

The family matter which I have to lay before you, is relative to dress; an article which you periodical speculatists have always made a particular object of your animadversion. Do not imagine, sir, that I trouble you merely to vent my spleen against some new fashion, that I have discovered some unforeseen inconveniences in the leaving off hoops, or mean to declaim against the immodesty of going without stays. I do not care one farthing whether petticoats are long or short, stomachers high or low, or whether the innumerable yards of rich stuff are employed in trimming or flouncing, or in sweeping the ground. I have no quarrel or concern with the vagaries of the fashion; all I complain of is the exorbitant expence of a woman's dress, let the fashion be what it will; an expence so enormous, that I can clothe myself and four boys from top to toe, for less than one third of the money, that goes to deck out my wife, who protests after all, to every other

woman

woman she sees, that she has not a gown to her back.

You must know, sir, that the greater part of my life has been spent in mercantile business, in which I got together a very considerable fortune, and which I was at last prevailed on to quit by my wife's continued remonstrances, that my application to it injured my health; though I must confess, I have scarce known a happy hour since I quitted my compting-house. Still, however, I consider, as every man ought, that a *shilling is a serious thing*, and keep a regular account of my family expences. Instead of allowing my wife *pin-money*, as it is called, I pay all her bills, milliners, mercers, &c. and carry them to the *bad* side of my accounts with my own hand; and it grieves me to the heart to see so much good money lavished away upon gew-gaws and frippery, things ten times worse than canvas, stay-tape, and buckram in a tailor's bill. Such a cloud of ruffles, double-ruffles, treble-ruffles, caps, aprons, and handkerchiefs! Such a deluge of gauze, muslin, blond, and Brussels lace! and then from Ludgate-Hill rich silks at so high a price! at the rate of ———I blush to own it——even of twenty shillings *per* yard! though, indeed, I remember when I could

could have purchased whole bales of the same sort for no more than three or four, till the coxcombs of my own sex enhanced the price, by making them up into fools-coats and birthday suits for themselves.

This, Sir, you will allow to be a heavy expence; yet, all this is nothing, absolutely nothing, in comparison to the grand object of my present application. After my wife's efforts at finery and magnificence had taken, as I supposed, their full swing, she made another stroke, which my folly and compliance has suffered her, by little and little, to carry to such an immoderate length, that this new piece of extravagance has cost me several thousand pounds in hard money. Unfortunately for me, a little scrub Jew, who called himself a merchant, because he carried on a sort of pedlar's traffick in jewels among his tribe, used to dine sometimes at my house, and soon contrived to talk my good woman into a taste for diamonds; a scrivener's wife too in the neighbourhood happened at that time to have jewels in her ears; so that, to humour my wife, little Tubal was ordered to furnish her with a pair of diamond tops, for so I think they called them. These, however, were scarce purchased, and the tops well fixt in her ears, before

before it was found indifpenfibly requifite to have bobs or drops to them, which alfo the infinuating Smoufe foon provided for her. The good humour which thefe occafioned, was but of fhort duration; for, alas, Sir, my wife foon told me, that thefe were but poor trumpery baubles, and at beft only fit for her *difhabille*; and, as a lady of quality had promifed to take her to court, it was abfolutely neceffary that fhe fhould have a pair of large handfome ear-rings; which by the help of our friend, fhe foon had, and which were fo very brilliant, and fet in fuch a fine tranfparent fafhion, that the countefs, who was to accompany her, turned pale with envy at the fight of them. Since then, Sir, I am afhamed to confefs to you, that I have been teazed and wheedled into giving her a diamond necklace, with an appurtenance dangling to it, which the charge in the bill has taught me to call *Efclavage*; and fince that again, a diamond girdle-buckle, a pair of diamond fhoe-buckles, a fprig made up of garnets and diamonds, and what provokes me worfe than all the reft, a diamond nofegay or *bouquet* (as fhe chriftens it) which comes to more than a younger child's fortune. Her affection for me has alfo induced her to wear my picture in miniature, fet round with diamonds,

diamonds, for a bracelet; befides which, her fingers are perfectly cramped with rings, fingle brilliants, hoop-rings, topazes and amethyfts without number. She has fcarcely the free motion of her knuckles and joints: they are placed five, fix, feven, or eight deep below one another, and it is abfolutely impoffible for her to wear more, unlefs, like the Indian women, fhe was alfo to bore her nofe.

This, Sir, is the groaning evil of my wife's drefs: and my cafe, which might once have been reckoned fingular, now becomes every day lefs and lefs uncommon. Formerly, indeed, rich jewels, as they fhine in the crown of monarchs, feemed alfo to be appropriated to thofe illuftrious characters, which approached neareft to that rank and dignity: but now they are worn indifcriminately by the wife of a duke or a city-deputy, by a princefs of the blood or a lady of pleafure. I can remember the time when women of an ordinary rank never dreamt of fuch extravagance, when they were contented with pebbles and pafte inftead of diamonds, wore French beads for pearls, and coloured glafs for precious ftones. At prefent every woman feems as familiar with diamonds as Cleopatra was of old; and to hear them boaft how cheap and plentiful they are grown of late years in England, one

would

would almoſt imagine, that they were inhabitants of Voltaire's good country of Eldorado, where (as I read lately in a tranſlation of his Candide) the ſoil conſiſted of gold, and diamonds lay, like ſtones and pebbles, in the ſtreets and highways.

My good wife is pleaſed at times to expatiate on the œconomy and good management of laying out money on theſe trinkets. They are, ſays ſhe, the only parts of dreſs, whoſe value remains undiminiſhed, and on which the coſt is not entirely thrown away. They have an intrinſick worth; and they, as well as plate, may be regarded as ſo much riches in bank, which, like a note, may be converted into caſh, whenever one pleaſes. This is fine talking truly! It is well known, that the ſetting, and the faſhion, and the like, come to above half the money that is paid for them; though indeed the expence is ſo great, taken altogether, that the buyer is often obliged to try the real value of his purchaſes by ſetting his jewels up to auction, and coining his plate, like the bankrupt Frenchman, into ſpecie. For my part I never ſee my wife in all her finery, without being immediately led to a contemplation of the immenſe ſums, which ſhe carries about her. When I conſider the common rate of intereſt, I cannot help calculating her ears,

ears, her neck, her hands, and her feet, each at ſo much *per annum*; and when I further reflect how much more *per cent*. I could have made of my money in the fair way of trade, ſhe ſeems to lie, like ſome cruel exciſe, upon my goods. A merchant can ſcarce ever afford to make a purchaſe even of Land, his whole principal being wanted to anſwer the demands of his buſineſs. How then can he ſupport the loſs of ſo much money lying dead on his wife's toilet? What profit can ariſe from her ear-rings or ſhoe-buckles? and where are his quick returns from her ſprig or her *bouquet*? ſhould he ſuffer a bill of exchange to be proteſted, in order to pay his lady's jeweller? or ſhould he run the riſk of ſeeing the precious ſtones themſelves in the hands of his aſſignees? An eſtate in land indeed will afford ſome profit to the owner of it: but the barren brilliants produce neither corn nor graſs, yield neither rent nor habitation, and ſerve no òne end (on this ſide of Temple-Bar at leaſt) except that of making the huſband poor, and the wife proud.

The bad effect which theſe ornaments have on the minds of the wearers, might furniſh no weak arguments againſt the uſe of them. So much finery muſt be ſhewn, and for what end does a woman
dreſs,

dress, unless it be in order to be seen? With what transport did my wife attend to the city scheme of an assembly at Haberdasher's-Hall! where, I dare say, her magnificence has since created no small disquiet in the family of many an alderman. I have already been reproached by more than one of the common council on this occasion, who have themselves shewn no more power to check this domestick evil than I exerted. They talk, however, very loudly of the imprudence of trusting a wife with such valuables: they tell me, it is absolutely putting an independent fortune into her hands. I have heard twenty stories of diamond-necklaces and aigrets being sent by distressed ladies to the pawnbroker's; and my attorney assures me, that he has the jewels of a lady of quality lying in his strong box, as a pledge for a thousand pounds lost at play, for which she had too much tenderness to trouble her husband. I have also heard another story of a lady who robbed herself, and prevailed on her kind husband to purchase for her a second time *her own* diamonds, new-set, of the jeweller, who had received the stolen goods at her hands.

You, Mr. Genius, seem to me to be something of a wag, and so perhaps you may laugh at my remonstrances; but in my mind it is a very serious affair,

affair, and deserves much consideration. To bring in a bill for some wise sumptuary law would perhaps not be quite unworthy the attention of the legislature. I consulted a serjeant at law some time ago on this head. He informed me, that, in the uncommon extent of his reading, he had met with a recital of one or two laws of this nature, but that they had been obsolete time out of mind. In one of these it was declared how many rows of lace a man might wear on his coat, according to his degree, from a duke to an esquire: and in another it was solemnly enacted, that no person, beneath the rank of a peer, should wear a coat so short as to shew his posteriors.

This, Sir, was the sum of the grave gentleman's counsel: hoping also some wholesome advice from you, or at least that my case may induce you to draw up a table of sumptuary laws for the benefit of the ladies, or, more properly speaking, for the benefit of their husbands, I remain,

SIR,

Your well-wisher and humble servant,

HUMPHRY GUBBINS.

My Little GENO!

I Have read your defcription of yourfelf with a deal of glee, and would give a thoufand pounds to-morrow to be juft fuch another tight little thing as you are. A fine fporting figure I warrant. How much do you weigh? Why did not you tell us that?—But no matter—I'll hold fix to one, you don't ride above nine ftone, faddle and bridle, and all together.

But hark ye, my little buck, the reafon of my writing to you at prefent is this. You muft know that I have laid Lord ——— a thoufand guineas, play or pay, with a good many bets depending on the fame lay, that I get a man to ride a little Yorkfhire galloway of mine, not thirteen hands and a half by Jupiter, five and twenty miles within the hour. I intended to ride myfelf, and have been in training for that end thefe fix weeks. But it won't do. I can't bring myfelf to lefs than twelve ftone three pounds and five ounces, do what I will. I have ufed exercife without meafure, eat fcarce any thing, and wore five flannel waiftcoats all the hot weather, and yet I am over weight after all. Now I'll tell you what, my little GENIUS; if you will ride for me, it is a *dead affair.*

affair. The minute you appear on the course, the odds I am sure, will run ten to one in my favour: so if you'll ride, you shall go halves in the wager. I'll bear you harmless from all losses; and if you have a mind for the job, and it is in your way, I'll recommend you to the jockey club as a proper man to make up the sportsman's calendar.

Your's,

Almack's, June 25.   J. F.

P. S. I have just read an account in the newspaper of the surprising little horse from Guadalupe, but two feet ten inches high, that is, just eight hands and an half. If you win my match for me, I will buy you this Guadalupe tit for your own riding.

*** *The original dates of the three first numbers of this paper having been inadvertently omitted, are inserted in this place, and are indeed a necessary part of periodical essays, in which many touches occur bearing particular reference to the time of their first publication. The Tatler and Spectator would often be obscure, and sometimes scarce intelligible, without this easy and familiar illustration.*

THE GENIUS. N° I. DATE. Thursday, June 11, 1761.
Ditto. N° II. DATE. Saturday, June 20, 1761.
Ditto. N° III. DATE. Tuesday, June 30, 1761.

THE GENIUS.
NUMBER IV.
Tuesday, July 13, 1761.

―――――*Pacifque imponere morem*   VIRGIL.

Receive, as War is like to ceafe,
Preliminary Thoughts on peace.

"WAR, faith Vincent Wing in his almanack, begets poverty, poverty peace." Now as fome, at leaft, of the parties engaged in the prefent conteft, feem to be nearly whirled round to that part of the circle of events, defcribed by the learned Philomath in the lines above-mentioned, all confiderate perfons begin to look forward to the confequences of fuch a revolution. The fagacious gentlemen at the Smyrna have already deliberated what part of our conquefts we fhall forego, and what we fhall retain. It was but the other day, that I faw a political junto in a corner of the room, with a map of America lying before them, and heard their final refolution not to reftore an acre of Canada; though they were a little disconcerted

disconcerted by a sugar-merchant from the city, who happened to drop in at the time, and declared with an oath, that the nation was undone, if we agreed to give up Guadalupe. The dealers in the stocks at Garraway's and Jonathan's are locking up all their ready money in the funds, and calculating at how much *per cent.* advance they shall be able to sell out on the proclamation of peace; and, in the mean time, some of the gentlemen at Arthur's, with many other persons at both ends of the town, are attentively considering the consequences of a peace in diminishing or increasing the emoluments of their several places, employments, or professions. A friend of mine, a very honest gentleman, who is an agent in the city, told me last week, that, if he was but so happy as to see the war continue for *only* four years more, he should make an estate, and ride in his coach and six: and it was but the next day that another intimate acquaintance, who has an employment in the war-office, declared to me, that he should lay down his chariot immediately upon a peace. For my own part, none of the various considerations, just enumerated, take hold on me. I have, I am sorry to say it, no money in the funds, and no employment under the government; and, as to politicks, since these are not times

when

when author-incendiaries are hired to take up the bellows to kindle the embers of sedition, or paid for laying them down again, what has a GENIUS to do with such considerations on the war or the peace? Libels, publick or private, are, alas!, attended only with fines, imprisonment, and the pillory. Waving, therefore, all other reflections, I shall consider this important event, come when it may, as a mere moralist; and endeavour to trace out the most probable effects of a peace, on the manners and principles of the good people of Great Britain.

I think, I may venture to prognosticate, that its first visible effects will be manifest in our dress, so that every lady and gentleman may be said to carry about them a kind of badge of peace and reconciliation, by adopting that foreign air, of which we are so great admirers. I have no apprehension that our home manufactures will stand still, and that the industrious artists of Spital-fields, whom publick spirit has of late so much encouraged, will be left to starve for want of due employment; but I think I foresee a whole pacquet of tailors, hair-cutters, and milliners, coming over in every vessel, and new patterns for caps and handkerchiefs, with the true Paris cut for cloaths, sent by every mail. There
seems

seems to have been much decency and chaste reserve in the habit of both sexes during the war; but, as we are allowed to be a very imitative, though not an inventive nation, I have some dread of the new fashions to be introduced after the peace. Then, perhaps, we may again see, among the ladies, uncovered shoulders, naked breasts, and legs revealed above the ancle; and among the men, short jerkins, white hats, and red-heeled shoes. In order to prevent these and other irregularities, I would humbly propose that, before the treaty is concluded, a congress of dressers, friseurs, and tyrewomen, plenipotentiary, be appointed to meet in some neutral country; and that, in the mean time, wooden dolls, dressed, *a la mode de Païs*, be reciprocally sent over between the cities of London and Paris, the better to adjust the preliminaries.

The large cargoes of tailors, &c. which the peace will waft over, will, however, be very inadequate to the number of English gentlemen, and *Milors Angloises*, that will immediately set sail for France, not for the sake of interest, but dissipation. A bridge from Dover to Calais would perhaps hardly render the emigrations of our people more frequent. Paris will then be considered as an addition to the number of our places of publick resort,

resort, and visited with as much readiness as Tunbridge, Bath, or Scarborough. This is a field which affords so much room for observation, that perhaps I may think it worth while to collect my materials on the spot, and may date some of my future papers from a Hotel at Paris. In the mean time, as our ministry and parliament will undoubtedly turn their thoughts towards the reduction of the national debt, necessarily increased by an expensive, though glorious war, my skill in politicks cannot suggest a better measure or more equitable tax to their consideration, than an heavy duty on the exportation of fools.

The ladies, who have justly complained of the dearth of men during the war, will, I dare say, concur with me in the propriety of this new tax, and to oblige them I would propose that all importations of volunteers from abroad, and other recruits, may be permitted duty-free. At the same time I cannot but congratulate my fair countrywomen on the great plenty of males, which the peace must produce. We shall no longer see a row of disconsolate females, sitting, like superannuated maidens, unsollicited at a ball, or a lady of fashion reduced to the necessity of *figuring in* with the butler. The officers of disbanded regiments will be glad to supply the deficiencies of half pay by the acceſſion of a large portion with a wife; and the brave gentlemen of the militia, no longer embodied or traverſing the country to diſtant encampments, will add to the publick meetings and aſſemblies of their own counties the brilliancy of a red coat and cockade, without the terror that ſuch a dreſs commonly brings with it, and as much harmleſſneſs as a ſword in the ſcabbard. Theſe new-commiſſioned ſoldiers may rejoice at the thought of having wiped off the contempt, that once cleaved to the name of MILITIA, and the ladies may be happy to take an hero to their arms, who can fight for his country, without being ſent out of it. In a word, this is one of the moſt jocund ideas, that peace affords. Bath, Briſtol, Margate, Brighthelmſtone, &c. will again become the ſcenes of pleaſure and delight; and the gallant warriors, who have deſerved ſo well of Mars, now devoted to Venus in her turn, have nothing to do but to recommend themſelves to the favour of the fair ſex, and endeavour to repair the ravages of war by determining, with captain Plume, *" To raiſe recruits the matrimonial way."*

But the joy, which the gaiety of theſe contemplations inſpires, is much allayed by conſidering the

the unhappy fituation of the daily, weekly, morning, and evening retailers of news. During the time of war, a battle in Germany, a fort ftormed in the Weft-Indies, or a Nabob created in the Eaft, is worth forty fhillings to every paper, that reprints the particulars from the Gazette Extraordinary: nay a town taken or a town loft is equally to the advantage of thefe half-fheet hiftorians; and the perpetual curiofity kept alive by the publick anxiety, fells off whole quires of uninterefting details of births, deaths, marriages, and bankruptcies. How great then muft be the dread of the confequences of peace to the proprietors of the fwarm of Advertifers, Gazetteers, Ledgers, Journals, Chronicles, and Evening Pofts? A peace, which will lie heavier on their papers than the double duty on the ftamps! My good friend Mr. H. BALDWIN of White Friars has already expreft to me his fears on this occafion. He fairly tells me to my face, that though the GENIUS were to ftand in the front of his paper three times a week, the publick attention would flag without great incidents and alarming paragraphs. He further acquaints me that, in order to recommend the St. James's Chronicle, he has engaged an ingenious gentleman, who, befides tranflating the mails, touching up collectors'

collectors' paragraphs, and writing occasional letters from the Hague, has also a sufficient portion of invention and philosophy, (having finished his education at St. John's college, Cambridge) to draw up accounts of earthquakes, meteors, and eruptions of Ætna and Vesuvius. Notwithstanding all this, he requires my further assistance. These, I protest, are matters with which I am very little acquainted; yet, I will strive (to use the news-paper phrase) to *establish correspondences* of another sort. I will use my interest to oblige the publick, like Boccalini, with the freshest advices from Parnassus; or, if my intelligence from that quarter should fail, I hope at least to be able, as well as some of my cotemporaries, to produce a dialogue from among the dead.

Flectere si nequeo superos, Acheronta movebo.

The happiest circumstance which I can recollect in favour of these persons employed in the eternal continuation of modern history, is, that a peace gives consequence and dignity to several events, which would be sunk and neglected during the tumult of a war. We all remember to have seen the whole nation, at such a period, split into parties concerning the possibility of a servant girl's subsisting for a month on a few crusts of bread and a pitcher

pitcher of water, while the wits of the age drew their pens, and were ready to spill their last drop of ink on each side of the question. At such a period a rabbit-woman, or a fortune-teller, a quack, or a bottle conjurer, engages the attention and engrosses the conversation of the whole town: and a quarrel between a dancer and his mistress, or a dispute between a couple of opera-singers, is of as much importance as the dissention between two generals. The violence of the British spirit of party will always create fuel for its own flame to feed upon: when it can no longer rage abroad, it will commit devastations at home; when it has no occasion to exert itself in vindication of liberty and property, it will vent itself on trifles; and the politicians of Britain, like the patriots of Lilliput, will divide concerning the height of shoe-heels, or the manner of breaking of eggs.

Among these domestick considerations, there is one in particular, which presses on my mind; but though I feel its force, I am quite at a loss to express my sensations: the idea is indeed too big and lofty, and so far above the pitch of these mean essays, that I seem, like the poet of old, to receive an admonition from some superior, to have recourse to more familiar subjects. I shall, therefore, leave to some greater master the endeavour to give to posterity the portrait of a KING, happy in the love and admiration of his subjects, proud of calling every Briton his fellow-countryman, and employed in cultivating THE ARTS of PEACE.

THE GENIUS.

NUMBER V.

Thursday, August 6, 1761.

Ergo ubi me in montes et in arcem ex urbe removi,
Quid prius illustrem? ——— HOR.

Far from the town, reviv'd by country air,
What country matters first demand my care?

AT this season of annual migration, (as a great writer solemnly stiles it) when the noble lord and the knight of the shire go down to their several seats, to support their interest in the county; when the lawyer takes his circuit; when the right reverend diocesan appoints his visitation; and when the humble out-rider, astride his saddle-bags, goes his rounds for fresh orders to dealers and chapmen in the country; —in a word, when business or pleasure carry thousands out of town, it is no wonder that one

or

or the other fhould have tranfported the GENIUS almoft two hundred miles beyond the limits of the bills of mortality. I could oblige the reader with a curious detail of my journey and adventures: I could tell him, that my publifher furnifhed me with one horfe, and my printer with another, together with his devil in livery, for an attendant: but thefe and many other curious particulars muft be deferred to fome future opportunity, that in the mean time I may have leifure to communicate fome few obfervations made, *en paffant*, on my fellow-fubjects refident in the country.

Notwithftanding the encomiums on a rural life, fown fo thick in the writings of poets and philofophers, we do not, in this degenerate age, think ourfelves fure to breathe the pure air of innocence and ancient fimplicity, the minute we have got out of the fmoke of London; we do not perceive a gradual declenfion of vice at every mile-ftone, or difcover morality upon every haycock. The clown who works at plough and cart, nay even the tender of fheep, for whom we have fo much refpect in paftoral and romance, excite our veneration little more than a linkboy or a hackney-coachman. The very milkmaid, with her pail on her head, engages our efteem no more than

than her fellow-labourers, who carry the yoke, about our streets: and so little do we expect to find the manners of the golden age prevail among our rusticks, that we see, without remorse or surprise, some bumkin Phillis condemned to the gallows for the murder of her bastard child, or a refractory Damon committed to the house of correction, set in the stocks, or sent abroad for a soldier.

But though we have surmounted these prejudices, perhaps we still retain some antiquated ideas of the manners of the country, scarce less remote from those which at present reign there, than even the manners of Arcadia. We are apt to take it for granted, that there yet remains among them, a strong leaven of that roughness and rusticity, which was so long considered as their distinguishing characteristick. It is scarce half a century ago, since the inhabitants of the distant counties were regarded as a species, almost as different from those of the metropolis, as the natives of the Cape of Good Hope. Their manners, as well as dialect, were entirely provincial; and their dress no more resembling the habit of the town, than the Turkish or Chinese. But time, which has inclosed commons, and ploughed up heaths, has likewise cultivated the minds, and

improved

improved the behaviour of the ladies and gentlemen of the country.. We are no longer encountered with hearty flaps on the back, or preft to make a breakfaft on cold meat and ftrong beer ; and in the courfe of a tour of Great Britain, you will not meet with a high-crowned hat, or a pair of red ftockings. Politenefs and tafte feem to have driven away the horrid fpectres of rudenefs and barbarity, that haunted the old manfion-houfe and its purlieus, and to have eftablifhed their feats in the country.

It is certainly to the intercourfe between the town and country, of late fo much more frequent, that this extraordinary change muft be imputed. Every traveller, that goes down to Cumberland or Cornwall, carries in fome fort the town along with him, and inevitably leaves fome tincture of it behind him : and every vifit, which an honeft ruftick pays to London, infenfibly files off fome of the ruft of the country. Formerly indeed, when *that the roads were dark, and ways were mire,* as Milton expreffes it in one of his fonnets, a journey into the country was confidered as almoft as great an undertaking as a voyage to the Indies. The old family coach was fure to be ftowed, according to Vanburgh's admirable defcription of it, it, with all sorts of luggage and provisions; and perhaps in the course of the journey, a whole village, together with their teams, were called in aid to dig the heavy vehicle out of the clay, and to drag it to the next place of wretched accommodation, which the road afforded. Thus they travelled, like the caravan over the deserts of Arabia, with every disagreeable circumstance of tediousness and inconvenience. But now, the amendment of the roads, with the many other improvements of travelling, have in a manner opened a new communication between the several parts of our island. The people venture forth, and find themselves enabled to traverse the country with ease and expedition. Stage-coaches, machines, flys, and post-chaises are ready to transport passengers to and fro between the metropolis and the most distant parts of the kingdom. The lover now can almost literally *annihilate time and space*, and be with his mistress, before she dreams of his arrival. Even a troop of geese and turkies may be driven from the country to town in a shorter time, than a nobleman and his family could have taken the journey heretofore, and the gamester offers to bet, that he can go from London to Edinburgh in twelve hours. In short, the manners,

fashions,

fashions, amusements, vices, and follies of the metropolis, now make their way to the remotest corners of the land, as readily and speedily along the turnpike road, as, of old, Milton's SIN and DEATH, by means of their marvellous bridge over the Chaos, from the infernal regions to our world.

The effects of this easy communication, have almost daily grown more and more visible. The several great cities, and we might add many poor country towns, seem to be universally inspired with an ambition of becoming the little Londons of the part of the kingdom wherein they are situated: the notions of splendor, luxury, and amusement, that prevail in town, are eagerly adopted; the various changes of the fashion exactly copied; and the whole manner of life studiously imitated. The country ladies are as much devoted to the card-table, as the rest of the sex in London; and being equally tired of making puddings and tarts, or working screens and carpets, they too have their routes, and croud as many of their neighbours as they can get together, into their apartments: they too, have their balls and concerts by subscription; their theatres, their mall, and sometimes their rural Ranelagh, or Vauxhall. The reading female hires her novels
from

from some country circulating library, which consists of about an hundred volumes, or, is trundled from the next market town in a wheelbarrow; and the merchant, or opulent hardware-man, has his villa three or four miles distant from the great town where he carries on his business. The nobleman and country squire, no longer affect an old-fashioned hospitality, or suffer the locusts of the country to eat them up, while they keep open house, and dispense victuals and horns of beer, like the ancient convents, to all comers; but more fashionably display the elegance of their taste, by making genteel entertainments: the same French cooks are employed, the same wines are drank, the same gaming practised, the same hours kept, and the same course of life pursued in the country as in town. The force of this illustrious example influences the whole country; and every male and female wishes to think and speak, to eat and drink, and dress, and live, after the manner of people of quality in London.

There is no popular subject of satire, on which the modern common places of wit and ridicule have been exhausted with more success, than on that of a mere cockney affecting the pleasures of the country. The dusty house close to the road side,
the

the half-acre of garden, the canal no bigger than a
wafh-hand bafon, &c. have all been marked out
with much humour and juftice; but after all, it
is not unnatural for a tradefman, who is continu-
ally pent up in the clofe ftreets and alleys of a po-
pulous city, to wifh for frefh air, or to attempt
to indulge a leifure hour in fome rural occupation;
and he who prevails on himfelf to give up the en-
joyments which nature has thrown into our laps in
the country, for a poor imitation of the follies
of the town, is infinitely more ridiculous. Ly-
curgus paffed a law in Sparta to prevent the impor-
tation of foreign vanities, and not only exprefsly
forbad the continuance of ftrangers in the city, for
fear of their corrupting the people, but for the
fame reafons would not permit his own people to
travel. Frequent intercourfe will undoubtedly produce fimilarity of manners; but the prefent communication between the various quarters of our
iflands, are fo far from being to be lamented, that
it is only to be wifhed and recommended, that they
may produce real refinements and improvements
of a valuable nature. At the fame time let it
be confidered by our country gentlemen and ladies, that no benefit can arife from changing one
fet of follies for another; and that the vices of the
town never appear fo truly ridiculous, or fo
thoroughly

thoroughly contemptible, as when they are aukwardly practised in the country.

The GENIUS.
NUMBER VI.
Thursday, August 20, 1761.

Atque ita mentitur, *sic veris falsa remiscet,*
Primo ne medium, medio ne discrepet imum.   Hor.

Slander and seeming, in the tale so mixt,
A thousand lies, and some small truths betwixt,
From end to end so cunning and compact,
'Tis hard to part the falshood from the fact.

SLANDER is an elegant and refined art, which has been brought to such a wonderful perfection, that it is not only universally practised and thoroughly understood, but is become the soul of polite conversation, and one of the most agreeable amusements of private life. Formerly, an infant lye, fearful of detection, and almost ashamed to shew itself in publick, made its way but slowly in the world; but now, the grossest falshood comes abroad with the utmost confidence, and peremptorily challenges our notice and attention. Not content with a general assertion of
any

any fact, it delights to be minute and circumstantial; enters into particulars, tells you the manner how, the time when, the place where, and gives the names of all the parties concerned. Such a report having gone round to every coffee-house, and got into every private family, having been universally told, and almost as universally credited, comes at last to the ears of the persons, who have been the unconscious subjects of it. Then the whole story proves entirely groundless; but they, whose reputation has been thus sported with, have no remedy except the consciousness of their own integrity, unless they chuse to make a genteel retaliation on their next neighbour, or to encounter with the air. It might be deemed too severe an act of censorial authority, to discountenance so polite an entertainment, and might, perhaps, put some of the best company to silence. Yet, since it is but of late that slander has, at its very birth, come forth (like Pallas from the head of Jupiter) armed at all points, hedged round with circumstance, and lackered over with probability, it may not be incurious to enquire, who are these active ministers of falshood, that set it so firmly on its legs, and bring it so early to maturity: I shall therefore dedicate the present paper to the

description

description of two of these ingenious characters, each of which rough draughts, the reader, who is at all conversant with the world, will, I am sure, be able to apply to more than one original.

Lady Jacyntha Scandal is a woman of the first fashion, and her house is the daily resort of the first company. Her reputation, it is true, is not quite unstained; but the blemishes of her character, like the spots in the sun, are overcome by the splendor of her quality. By the force of a genteel malice and pleasant ill-nature, together with an happy assurance that enables her to throw off the reserve of her sex, she is universally acknowledged to be a wit. The smartness of her repartees bespeaks uncommon vivacity, and her exquisite turn for the *double Entendre* denotes an admirable pruriency of imagination. She will tell a story to a room full of mixt company, almost rich enough in its circumstances for the high-wrought memoirs of a woman of pleasure, without using one indelicate expression, without offending the chastest ear, or betraying the least consciousness that she is all the while on the very brink of indecorum. She receives all her visitors with the most perfect good breeding; but the instant that any one of them departs, he becomes

the

the subject of her pleasantry and ridicule to those that stay behind. She cannot raise our idea of her own character, but she can lessen our opinion of another's. In a word, her ladyship is the fear and delight, the envy and scorn, the honey and gall, of the great world : nobody thinks well of her, but nobody speaks ill of her, and every body visits her.

Neither love, nor honours, nor riches, nor any other worldly pleasure, can give half so much delight to LADY JACYNTHA SCANDAL, as the gratification of her dear passion for mischief: and there are likewise certain other female geniusses, who love a little witty malice better than their prayers. Several of these are frequently assembled at LADY JACYNTHA'S, and it is to the ingenuity of this petticoat junto that the strange reports, which alarm the whole town, are often owing. They are not contented with the more than usual poignancy of their chit-chat over the tea-table, but set themselves to invent important slanders, and to devise the surest means to give them colour. If some pale-faced London coquette, some hagged member of the cabal, worn to the bone with paint and late hours, is offended with the ruddy bloom of some new toast from the country, it is here that

that she meditates revenge, and it is suddenly proclaimed, or, as the phrase is, *reported*, that the innocent young lady has been detected in the grossest familiarities with one of her father's footmen; or if a dutchess has piqued some of the junto, by excluding them from her route, or leaving them uninvited to a ball, her rank will so little avail to exempt her from the like treatment, that the slander will rather be aggravated in proportion to the dignity of its object.

Never did statesman study more attentively the art of political lying, or stockjobber use more stratagems to raise or sink the value of the funds, than are used by the ingenious junto, to send forth an injurious report with secrecy. Nobody knows on what authority the story is founded which every body repeats; and it is as impossible to trace the slander up to its source, as to discover the head of the Nile. I have observed, indeed, that it commonly takes its rise in the most distant quarter, from that where the parties reside whom it is intended to affect. When a person of high rank is destined for the victim, an emissary is dispatched to set the story abroad at some obscure coffee-house in the city, whence it speedily marches to its head quarters near the court: or,

if perhaps some rich banker and his family are to be made a sacrifice, it is whispered about the politer part of the town, that a certain great house near the Royal Exchange has stopt payment. Sometimes the curious tale seems to have travelled out of the country, and sometimes, like the great fire of London, it breaks out in several quarters of the town at once. However, come whence it may, true or false, probable or improbable, down it goes; and the dear, witty, sweet, mischievous creatures, who invented it, practise ten thousand additional little arts to give it credit. " They do
" not believe, indeed, that the thing happened,
" just as it is related; but then there *must* be *some-*
" *thing* in it, say what they will, or else how
" could there be such a number of *particulars?*
" They have heard too, (good souls!) nay,
" they *know*, that the parties themselves are very
" uneasy at the story, and have taken a great
" deal of pains to discredit it, which looks very
" suspicious; for why should they be so concerned,
" if, (*in part* at least) it were not true, or suffer
" their peace to be broken by a mere idle report?"
With such candour and humanity do. LADY JACYNTHA, and the rest of these good sort of people express their sentiments; and at the same

time many of the moſt intimate friends of the perſons reviled repeat the ſlander, or at leaſt make no efforts to contradict it : yet where is the offence or injury ? it was not their invention, you know, and they only joined in the common *talk of the town.*

Lord Bacon ſomewhere remarks that great inquiſitiveneſs and curioſity concerning the affairs of others, is one of the chief characteriſticks of envy. It would be unpardonable to attribute ſo black a paſſion to a fine lady; and yet it is certain, that no mortal was ever more ſtrongly poſſeſſed of that inquiring ſpirit than LADY JACYNTHA SCANDAL. She will hold long conferences, for the ſake of intelligence, with her mantua-maker or milliner, and has an admirable knack at drawing the ſecrets of families from ſervants and children. By theſe, and the like means, ſhe is acquainted with the private buſineſs and private pleaſures of the whole town. Nobody knows ſo well as her ladyſhip, what lady's diamonds are in pawn, what duke's eſtate was lately mortgaged, what lord's ſiſter's fortunes are not paid off, what poet keeps a miſtreſs, what young man and woman are clandeſtinely married, or what grave judge has been caught, in a frolickſome vein, at

a game

a game of romps with his cook-maid. Such are the anecdotes which she is eager to learn; and her affiduity in collecting them is only to be equalled by her industry in making them publick.

Equally attached to slander, but of the other sex, and of a lower rank, is the pert, volatile, prating, scribbling, JACKY TATTLE. JACKY is the son of an attorney of Furnival's-Inn, and was originally intended for his father's profession; but the strength of his Genius soon drew him from the desk, and carried him amongst under-actors, under-authors, and women of the town: in which company he soon converted his pertness into assurance, and wonderfully improved his natural talents for lying and defamation. Slander may, indeed, be said to be his passion, and to spread it his daily employment; and as birds are observed to peck the finest fruit, so this fluttering tom-tit always aims his petulant attacks at the fairest characters. The company with which he associates, naturally deal in detraction, his folly induces him to give credit to the slander, and his vanity often urges him publickly to interfere in it. He is also a great writer of anonymous epistles from unknown friends, as well as incendiary letters from secret enemies. He sometimes amuses himself with sending letters and paragraphs to the newspapers, in which he sometimes appears as a six-lined epigrammatist, and is confidently said to be the author of several articles in The New Review. If ever you observe an impertinent fellow, in the next box at a coffee-house, listening to your private conversation with a friend, or casting his eye over a letter, which you are reading or writing, that is JACKY TATTLE: —Or if you see a strange town-fly fluttering at the play-house, staring every body out of countenance, and buzzing about the theatre, now in the orchestra, now in the green-boxes, and by-and-by behind the scenes, that is JACKY TATTLE.— Poor JACKY's courage is unhappily not quite adequate to his malignity, so that his indiscretions have sometimes betrayed him into punishment for his slanders; yet his appetite for detraction must be gratified; he considers himself as a formidable adversary to several characters of merit, and is thoroughly persuaded that the ladies all believe him to be a wit and a fine gentleman.

THE GENIUS.

NUMBER VII.

Tuesday, September 1, 1761.

Hic Vir, hic est! tibi quem promitti sæpius audis,
Augustus Cæsar! Divûm Genus! aurea condet
Sæcula qui rursus Latio. ——— VIRG.

This, this is HE, whom rolling years shou'd bring,
Augustus Cæsar, sprung from Gods, our King;
Doom'd to waft blessings to this happy shore,
And in our times the Golden Age restore!

NOTWITHSTANDING the rigour of some criticks, which would entirely preclude the choice of temporary subjects, there are no parts of periodical publications, which have been more favourably received at their first appearance, or afforded more entertainment afterwards, than such as were founded on matters merely fugitive, and peculiar to the time in which they were written. Such pieces become a kind of supplement to history: they furnish the curious with anecdotes; and it is from these materials, that the literary virtuoso collects the manners, fashions, and customs

customs of his ancestors. The Tatlers and Spectators, for instance, serve almost as effectually as a gallery of pictures, to shew the habits in vogue at that period; and are, at the same time, a kind of historical register of the prevailing pleasures, and the objects of publick attention. In the perusal of these papers we seem to be endued, like Janus, with a sort of backward face that enables us to take a clear, retrospective view of times past. We spend evenings at the clubs of our fathers, some of whom may perhaps have been Mohocks, and gain admittance to the toilets of our mothers and grandmothers. We read, not without satisfaction, comments on the performances of actors, whom we never saw: we look upon the celebrated trunk-maker with a veneration equal to that of his cotemporaries; and are hugely entertained at Powell's puppet-shew.

It is to be considered, that periodical writers converse more familiarly with the publick than any other authors; they are allowed, nay expected, to chat of themselves, the play, the opera, and are even in danger of being neglected, if they omit to discourse on the popular topicks of conversation. Our good advice (for we are all sagacious monitors of the publick) must not be

obtruded

obtruded on our readers, but muſt ſeem to be uſhered in by the occaſion, and to take its colour from the times. The preſent complection of the people is ſuch, that I find it abſolutely vain and ridiculous to attempt writing to them on any other ſubject than that of the Royal Wedding and Coronation. My printer too has moſt earneſtly requeſted me to give what he calls *a touch on the times*, and to ſay ſomething on theſe great occaſions. He tells me, that there is ſcarce one of his cuſtomers, who would not ſooner give a guinea for a night's lodging on the floor at Greenwich, or five for the ſake of ſitting eight and forty hours in Weſtminſter Abby, than part with two-pence halfpenny for *the* GENIUS, unleſs it treats of thoſe ſolemnities. Scarce a paragraph of news, relating to any other matters, will go down. The proceedings of the Court of Claims, the ladies coronation robes, and the aldermens' coronation wigs, furniſh out the moſt intereſting articles of intelligence. The maſter of an ale-houſe in the next lane to my apartments has hung out a paper lanthorn to advertiſe the neighbourhood, that he ſells the beſt Mecklenburg purl and Coronation porter. The theatres are, I doubt not, both employed in the preparation of entertainments

ſuitable

suitable to the splendor and joy of these happy celebrities; and a famous field-preacher has, to my knowledge, already anticipated the Archbishop in a Coronation Sermon.

I have also lately been honoured with a pacquet of letters from several correspondents, not one of which but relates to these two grand occasions of festivity. Many, I find, are sollicitous to know what will become of *the* GENIUS, and into what corner he will squeeze his little body at the coronation. A gentleman, who signs himself Timothy Cautious, tells me, that in case I have no ticket, I may easily be conveyed into the hall undiscovered in some old countess's pocket, or be rolled up and overshadowed by the full bottom of a nobleman's periwig. A lady gives herself the trouble to recapitulate the advantages and disadvantages of my person on this occasion; and informs me that, indeed, I may be put any where, but that unfortunately, I shall be able to see no where. Another correspondent, who subscribes himself COKE *junior*, and dates from the Inner Temple, says, that he hopes I have secured a place in Westminster-hall, and adds (but I do not know what he means by it) that he should be glad to see me appear there oftener than I used to do. The two following letters

letters are, I think, the moſt proper of any I have received, to ſubmit to my readers at full length: to them therefore I ſhall devote the reſt of this paper.

The firſt comes from a lady, and is as follows,

To the GENIUS.

SIR,

I Have often lamented that I did not live in thoſe illuſtrious ages of the world, when our ſex was allowed to diſtinguiſh itſelf by acts of proweſs and chivalry. I ſhould have delighted to have traverſed the deſarts, and to have reſcued innocent virgins in diſtreſs. The degeneracy of the preſent times has often been the cauſe of my ſore affliction; and there is no circumſtance from which I have ever in my life reaped ſo much confolation, as from the thoughts of the approaching Coronation, which ſolemnity ſtill retains ſome leaven of the ancient manners of this kingdom; of which I can vouch no ſtronger teſtimony than the well-known ceremony of the CHAMPION in Weſtminſter-hall. But there is, however, even in this ſome deficiency, which I am ready and willing to ſupply. Since the King has graciouſly thought fit to adorn this high festival with the presence of a Queen, it is surely a dishonour to her merits, and an indignity to the whole sex, that one should be wanting to vindicate her beauty, when a champion appears to assert the rights of his majesty. Tilts, and jousts, and tournaments, were originally instituted almost entirely in honour of the ladies; and a total neglect of them in such ceremonies reflects disgrace on our national gallantry. A noble Spaniard would be shocked to think of it. To prevent this dishonour, and to preserve the glory of the nation, I do most humbly propose myself as a LADY CHAMPIONESS, and intend to enter the hall, properly accoutred, and properly attended, immediately after the departure of the Champion. I have already trained and disciplined a milk-white palfrey for this purpose, and mean to be attended with none other than *the* GENIUS for my DWARF: of which I hereby give you notice, that you invest yourself with suitable habiliments, and otherwise prepare yourself for this awful occasion.

THALESTRIS DYMOKE.

Given this thirtieth of August, 1761.

The other letter comes from a gentleman, who, I can aſſure the publick, *is no leſs a* GENIUS *than* MYSELF.

S I R, *Sept.* 2, 1761.

AT this critical conjuncture I cannot think, or talk, or write, of any thing but the wind. I gape at every weather-cock, and if there are none in ſight, am perpetually throwing up my handkerchief to ſee, if there be a fair wind for the paſſage of Her Intended Majeſty. I am a good deal of a valetudinarian, and would, in general, almoſt as ſoon wiſh for a plague as an Eaſterly wind; but now I pray for it every hour in the day. In ſhort, Sir, theſe thoughts have filled my brains ſo long, and poſſeſt themſelves ſo entirely of my imagination, that the wind has got up into my head, and is attended with all the ſymptoms of a poetical vertigo. Modern odes are, you muſt al-allow, the moſt flatulent of all compoſitions: you will not be ſurpriſed, therefore, that the Weſt Wind, which impregnated Virgil's mares, ſhould alſo make me teem with an ode, and here it is at your ſervice.

O D E

ODE TO A WEATHER-COCK.

O Thou, whom all the Zephyrs court,
  Who lov'st with every breeze to play,
      Changing,
      Ranging,
      Whirling,
      Twirling,
Veering a thousand times a day,
Why with a nation's wishes wilt thou sport?
  Observe, while here and there you fly,
  Where anxious GEORGE, with wishful eye,
    Watches each varying motion!
Then summon from the secret cell,
  Where Eastern breezes dwell,
Prosp'rous gales to fan the ocean!

Once, faith the Muse, great Æolus, who binds
  In chains the subject winds,
  Who rideth on their wings in storm,
  When hurricanes the deep deform;
Or hushes them to peace, and bids them sleep
  On the calm bosom of the deep,
  When the winds and waves are laid:—
This mighty God once lov'd a Northern maid.

While faithful to his Northern fair,
North winds alone poffeft the boundlefs air:
Pregnant with rage and ftorms no more,
Soft fighs and zephyrs in each gale they bore;
  While Love did in his bofom reign,
  Fixt, as the needle to the pole,
  True to the wifhes of his foul,
Still Northward pointed each obedient vane.

  Now then, when George and England call,
May he, the God that rules thee, deign to fmile!
And, his own love remembring, for a while,
  Each envious wind enthrall!
And now, as Circe for Ulyffes once, chain'd faft
  Each adverfe blaft!
EAST turn thy point! due EAST! that brings
  Its richeft treafure on its wings,
The Beft of Bleffings to the Beft of Kings!

THE GENIUS.
NUMBER VIII.
Thurſday, September 17, 1761.

―――― *Ordine gentis*
Mores, et ſtudia, et populos, et prælia dicam. VIRGIL.

The politicks, and morals, of the ſtate,
The people's various manners I'll relate.

THE learned and honourable truſtees of The Britiſh Muſeum, well knowing and duly conſidering the great work in which I am engaged, and thoroughly weighing the infinite importance of it to the morals of the people of Great Britain, have graciouſly reſolved to afford me every aſſiſtance in their power, and given orders to the proper officers for my conſtant admiſſion to the reading-room, with free leave to peruſe ſuch old papers and ſcarce manuſcripts, as my curioſity may lead me to look into. They have alſo further ſhewn themſelves ſo favourably inclined to me and my undertakings, that they have ſet a-part a certain angle of the

room

room for my particular ufe; wherein there is erected an elegant machine, curioufly contrived by Mr. Burnet, cabinet-maker in the Strand, and known by the name of *the* GENIUS's reading-defk. This machine, in confideration of my diminutivenefs, is conftructed fomewhat on the principles of that ufed by Gulliver in Brobdignag, and has often enabled me to manage the moft unwieldy volumes with eafe, as well as, by means of its fteps, to climb up to the top of the page of many a tall folio. The modern artificers of furniture have cultivated no tafte in moveables with more fuccefs, than that which they call *the* BOOK FASHION; which is an ingenious method of reducing tea-chefts to the fhape and femblance of octavos and duodecimos, as well as *Bedes* and other *neceffary* utenfils, of a larger fize, to the figure of quartos and folios. Thefe goods may be had, neatly gilt and lettered, at the warehoufe of any fafhionable upholfterer; but where could fuch a mode be followed with fuch ftrict propriety as in the conftruction of the implements of Literature? On your firft entrance into the room, you would take *the* GENIUS's reading defk for an irregular heap of books of different fizes, thrown carelefsly one upon another: and, as it is ufual to preferve fome analogy between the

mock

mock volumes and the moveable which takes their form, commonly appropriating. Pope's Letters, the Spectators, &c. to the tea-table, and *waste paper* histories, &c. to the *closet*; in like manner the artist has ingeniously raised the steps of my desk upon STATIUS, and SCALIGER, and UP-*ton*, and STEP-*ney*, and MOUNT-*eny*, &c. with many other curious conceits of the like nature, not unworthy the genius of an upholsterer. A waggish Cantab, who popt into the room the other day, after having examined the desk with great attention, told me, that he found *the* GENIUS, like Bayes, had certain mechanical helps for wit, and christened it (after the university stile of punning) my *Gradus ad Parnassum*.

A few days ago, as I was studiously employed at this desk, and preparing to say a word or two to the publick, as it were, *ex cathedrâ*, a sagacious friend of mine, belonging to the Museum, (who is for ever peering with his pur-blind eyes into some curiosity, or brushing with his learned nose the dust from some rare manuscript) threw a bundle of papers before me. This choice pacquet appeared, upon examination, to have been formerly in the possession of Sir Thomas More, our great chancellor, of worthy and facetious memory, to whom

whom it was addreffed by Petrus Ægidius (or, as fome tranflators call him, Peter Giles) of Antwerp, the very perfon to whom the chancellor infcribed his Hiftory of UTOPIA. This manufcript contains a full detail of the laws, manners, cuftoms, &c. of the inhabitants of the ifland of ANEMOLIA, taken from memory by Petrus Ægidius, like Sir Thomas More's own narrative, from the relation of Raphael. This country, as well as feveral others mentioned in thefe papers, is, I find, taken notice of in the Utopia; and Sir Thomas, fpeaking curforily of the people, calls them *fuperbi magis quam fapientes*, a proud rather than a wife nation. My veneration for manufcripts is not fo implicit as to think, with fome antiquarians, that every old paper is worthy to be printed, which has not yet been in print: but as I look upon this to be of an extremely curious nature, I fhall put it to the prefs with all convenient fpeed; and my friend abovementioned has, for the benefit of the illiterate, chearfully fubmitted to the labour of a tranflation. This valuable narrative is written originally, like the Utopia, in very elegant Latin; and the genuine papers, for the fatisfaction of the Virtuofi, fhall lie, till the time of publication, at Mr. Becket's, bookfeller, in the Strand. In the mean time, I have thought proper to amuse my readers with the following extracts made here and there from different parts of this valuable work, and I believe that most persons will readily concur with me, merely from this specimen, that ANEMO-LIA, must be the most extraordinary country under the sun.

" *Anemoliorum lingua, suavior auditu, verbis abundantior, fidelior animi interpres, mutila: ipsi autem, &c.*"   Apud M. S.

THERE is no language in the world more sweet, more copious, and better adapted to express the meaning of the speaker, than that of the ANEMOLIANS: and yet, what is very wonderful, the ANEMOLIANS themselves never make use of it in conversation; but having discarded their own native tongue, just after it had arrived to its highest pitch of perfection, they have, by a kind of general infatuation, adopted the harsher dialect of their neighbours and natural enemies, the ACHORIANS. The children of the lowest artificers are early instructed in the Achorian language, and are much ashamed, if they happen, by chance, to express themselves in their mother-tongue. From this strange national folly the ACHORIANS have

assumed

assumed an air of great superiority, and affect to regard the ANEMOLIANS as little better than barbarians. So very unaccountable, and yet so deeply rooted, is this contempt for their native language, that during the short time I sojourned among them, a grammar of its rudiments and principles was burnt by the common hang-man; and a very ingenious author was condemned to be starved to death for having compiled an Anemolian Dictionary.

Their passion for literature, such as it is, is so violent, that the number of their publications is incredible. They have, indeed, among their ancient authors, several excellent writers on almost every subject, but these, like their language, are grown obsolete: for the ANEMOLIANS are such wonderful lovers of novelty, that they indulge a desire for literary trash, almost as intemperate and irregular as the longings of pregnant women, or rather like the false appetite of green-sickness girls for chalk, oatmeal, and unripe fruit. Several thousand printed sheets of paper are published every morning, as many at noon, and as many more every evening; besides which, a vast variety of thin volumes, containing certain sippets of philosophy, morality, and the arts, make their appearance with every new moon. But moſt of theſe hourly, daily, and monthly publications are calculated merely for the amuſement of the hour in which they come forth, and grow immediately afterwards as dull, uſeleſs, and unentertaining, as a laſt year's almanack. Hence theſe publications are, in the phraſe of that country, very properly ſtiled *Periodical.* The art of writing is, indeed, nearly fallen into utter contempt among them, and become a mean handicraft buſineſs, and wretched manufacture. So venal a profeſſion is exerciſed by few or none of any reputation; whence it happens, that though their new books are almoſt innumerable, the number of their writers is exceedingly ſmall, four or five perſons being the ſole authors of every work in every ſcience; in each of which they acquit themſelves with equal dexterity.

The ANEMOLIANS affect an uncommon love for natural freedom; but their aim in this, as in moſt other particulars, appears to be mercenary, endeavouring to gain pecuniary advantages to themſelves by converting their *liberty* into *property.* According to theſe principles, the common inhabitants of every town and diſtrict within the kingdom ſet themſelves to publick ſale by auction, once in ſeven years; two or three, and ſometimes

four

four or five, or fix or feven, of fuperior rank, appear as purchafers at the fame place, on which occafions the higheft bidder is the buyer. By thefe means the venal commonalty often extort large fums, being paid for, like cattle, at fo much *per head*, and yet they have frequent caufe to repent of their bargain; though it is but common juftice to add, that the purchafers alfo frequently pay more for them than they are worth.

* * * * * * * * * * * * * *

P. S. Having proceeded thus far in tranf-lating the paffages I have felected from the M.S. I find that my extracts are too large to come within the compafs of one paper. I am therefore obliged to referve the reft, among which are many curious particulars relating to the ladies, for my next, with whch I fhall prefent the reader as foon as poffible.

THE GENIUS.

NUMBER IX.

Saturday, September 26, 1761.

Quod te per Genium, Dextramq; Deofq; Penates
Obfecro & obteftor, Vitæ me redde priori :
Qui fimul afpexit, quantum dimiffa petitis
Præftent, maturè redeat, repetatq; relicta.   HOR.

By heav'n, by all the love you pledged your wife,
Give, I conjure thee, give my former life!
Compare the prefent ills with comforts paft,
And be with your firft fortunes bleft as laft!

AS the following letter is the firft of any confequence, with which I have been favoured from a female hand, the preference due to a lady muft be my apology for deferring the reft of the manufcript, relating to *the Anemolians*, to my next paper.

To

To the GENIUS.

SIR,

WHEN I inform you, that I am juft raifed from the humble condition of plain Mrs. Greenfield to the honour of being the lady of a member of parliament; when I tell you, that my hufband was, at the laft general election, chofen by a great majority of voters for one of the moft eminent county-towns in the kingdom; when I further add, on good authority, that the petition intended to have been preferred againft him is withdrawn, and that he feems likely to fit out his feven years in the honourable Houfe of Commons; when I fend you, Sir, all this feeming good news, it only ferves to acquaint you, in other words, that I am one of the moft unhappy women upon earth; that my hufband is an undone man, and that my dear children, though born to fome eftate, are in danger of being thrown upon the wide world to earn their uncertain bread.

But that which adds the greater acutenefs to my mifery, is the fad and fudden revolution of our fortune; for we are not only hurried to certain deftruction, but drawn from a ftate of the moft perfect tranquillity.

tranquillity. I have now been married almost fourteen years. My husband always behaved to me with the truest tenderness and affection; the whole study of my life has been to promote his happiness; and our little family has, all that while, lived comfortably in a cheap country upon a very moderate fortune. But, alas! the late general election has entirely reversed our situation. You must know, Sir, that our county, like many others, is unhappily split into little parties and factions, and a perpetual contest is kept alive by the two most opulent persons in it, which of them shall have the credit with the great folks *above*, as the phrase is, of managing the rest. A noble peer in our neighbourhood, who is the person that carries on this important dispute with a wealthy baronet, did us the honour of a visit about a year ago, earnestly intreating my husband to appear with another gentleman, in his lordship's interest, as a joint candidate for the county-town, in opposition to two others supported by the baronet. My husband's vanity and ambition took the alarm in an instant, and he was all on fire for the honour of representing so respectable a place in parliament. Only two small objections presented themselves: the first was, that his property lying chiefly in the funds,

funds, his landed eftate did not quite amount to the yearly value, which, it feems, is required as a neceffary qualification : and the fecond was, that his property, taken all together, would by no means enable him to defray the numerous and heavy expences of a contefted election. Both thefe objections were, however, without much difficulty, furmounted. My hufband had, indeed, at firft, fome fcruples of confcience on the firft article, as neither he nor I could think it poffible for him to take the oath of qualification with his feat, without the requifite addition to his eftate. An eminent lawyer, fetched from the inns of court in London on purpofe, foon folved this difficulty, and made out a qualification in form, by means of an *hocus-pocus* conveyance from my lord to my hufband, by which, they tell me, that my hufband has enlarged his eftate, though I know too well that he has not added to his income. As to the fecond objection, that was immediately got over by his lordfhip's declaration, that he meant to defray the whole expence of the election himfelf. My hufband therefore chearfully prefented himfelf as a candidate; but I muft not forget to mention, that though he was brought in by the noble lord, as the whole country will tell you, *for nothing*, it coft cost us very near a thousand pounds. There were several unforeseen incident expences, created chiefly by the zeal of my husband's *best friends*, and those who were most warm in his interest; of which expences, as he seemed to be the immediate cause, though incurred without his direction, he was ashamed to carry in the bills to his lordship at the close of the contest, which had cost the parties, both together, above thirty times that sum.

But this loss, as it was the first, so it would have been the least, and most easily to be put up with, if my husband had been so fortunate as to have lost his election. I must repeat to you, Sir, that he was chosen by an indisputable majority; and I repeat it to you, not without sorrow; as I now too late discover the wisdom of the legislature, in demanding such a qualification in property, since I see that a large estate is necessary to keep up the consequence even of a dependent member, as well as to support the real dignity of independence. The change in my husband's situation is much less extraordinary than the alteration in his ideas. He is no longer contented with being a plain country gentleman, as heretofore, but considers himself as a kind of publick character. Our house is now thrown open to all comers and goers, and all the

honest

honeſt freemen muſt be indulged with the run of our cellar and kitchen. We have treated the worſhipful corporation more than once, and every private gentleman muſt be loaded with civilities in proportion to his influence and intereſt. My huſband was formerly of ſome uſe to the country, merely by acting in the commiſſion of the peace; but he has now, on the death of his lordſhip's brother, been appointed colonel of our militia; at our laſt aſſizes, he was unanimouſly choſen to be foreman of the Grand Jury; and now that his preſence is become of ſo much conſequence in the county, I know that he will think it indiſpenſibly requiſite for him always to fill the chair at the Seſſions. Theſe, and ſeveral other county-dignities, with which I plainly foreſee he will be honoured, will not be maintained without extraordinary expences, beſides thoſe which muſt inevitably attend the neceſſary journies between town and country.

From my mention of Journies, you will immediately conclude that we have an houſe in town. To take one was, indeed, the firſt reſolution which my huſband made after his election; and that we are already in poſſeſſion of a very handſome houſe in one of the moſt faſhionable parts of the

the town, is no inconfiderable circumftance of my unhappinefs. We came to London time enough, you may be fure, to attend the Coronation; and feveral of the electors being drawn up to town by the fame great occafion, my hufband hired a room, at the price of an hundred guineas, for our own and their accommodation to fee the proceffion. " Thefe little acts of kindnefs, my dear, (fays he to me) done for a fmall expence at a time when they appear difinterefted, go as far as twenty-fold that fum in feafons of commotion and diftrefs." Indeed nothing feems to terrify him fo much as the apprehenfions of being thought niggardly in his notions, and narrow in his œconomy. He has of late frequently reprehended me for the plainnefs of my drefs, and tells me, that the lady of a member of parliament, efpecially the reprefentative of a place of fo much confequence, ought to make a genteel appearance. I am in great fear of his prefenting me with fome jewels. He has already provided a fplendid equipage, and has put the fervants into laced liveries; and moreover infifts on our having a man-cook: " for, (fays he) I fhall often bring home fome of my brother members to dinner; and, you know, my dear, they are ufed to good living, and muft have their things well done."

As

As my hufband has hitherto always behaved in a prudent and reafonable manner, this ftrange extravagance would almoft perfuade me that he was out of his fenfes, if I did not fee that a foolifh infatuation, and I know not what idea of being in parliament, has feifed his mind. This, he tells me, is the crifis of his fortune, and that his fuccefs in his election will prove the making of his family. A feat in parliament he looks upon as a mere earneft of the honours which he is hereafter to enjoy. He affures me again and again, that the moft eminent perfons in the kingdom have rifen to their prefent dignities by the fole force of parliamentary talents; and that for his own part he has no doubt of making his way, now he has once got into the road of preferment. He feems fo fure to carry his point, that he even threatens to take no notice of any of his relations, but fuch as fhall fhew him due attention and refpect; and he has juft determined to fend our eldeft boy, who is about nine years of age, to Weftminfter School, becaufe he thinks he has difcovered in the lad fomething of an *oratorical* turn. I am very well-affured, from all his converfation and behaviour, that his vanity prompts him to believe that he fhall make himfelf of confequence in parliament; and I am very

very much afraid that he will open his mouth, almoſt immediately after he has taken his ſeat, and expoſe himſelf in publick; for I, who am partial to him, yet know him too well to imagine that any ſucceſs can attend his efforts to ſhine in eloquence or politicks. You may ſmile, perhaps, Sir, and think that I conſider the matter too minutely; but I am fully perſuaded, that he often means to try the ſtrength of his talents as a ſpeaker, on me and the little circle of familiar friends that drop in to viſit us. He takes up every thing in a ſtile of argument and authority, runs the eaſy chat of converſation into politicks, and talks with much vehemence for a long time together upon ſubjects which neither I, nor any of my female acquaintance, can at all comprehend. He tells me over and over, alone and in company, that there is a great ſcene opening upon us, that the commencement of a new reign, and a new parliament, muſt of courſe produce great events; and that thoſe who have the ableſt talents for the buſineſs of the houſe, will be the moſt certain to diſtinguiſh themſelves and reap the greateſt ſhare of honour and profit.

For my part, Sir, I am no Mrs. Weſtern, and pretend to no ſkill in politicks; neither am I of opinion, that a candidate's being poſſeſſed of wealth

enough

enough to bribe his conſtituents, ought to recommend him to their choice; but I am fully ſatisfied, that a conſiderable degree of poperty is neceſſary to his integrity, ſince, without it, the greateſt talents will not avail to preſerve his independence. My huſband, for example, publickly declares, and ſeems to affect a conſequence from it, that he ſhall always go with His Lordſhip: he ſeems, indeed, to be ſo involved in his parliamentary ſyſtem, that he has quite loſt ſight of his domeſtick œconomy. While he is bringing his vaſt ſchemes to bear, he will be every day haſtening his ruin. The ſucceſs, with which he is ſo elevated, is a piece of good fortune that brings deſtruction along with it; for what advantage can be derived from any preferment, which requires a man to make his expences amount to above double the value of his receipts? I can account eaſily enough for the manner in which we are to ſupport our way of living during the preſent year; and the ſame foreſight convinces me, that it will be abſolutely impoſſible for us to go through another. The follies of moſt married men are charged on their wives; but this, I am ſure, has, from firſt to laſt, been purſued, as well as undertaken, much againſt my conſent. It was with a heavy heart that I ſaw my huſband

enter

enter into this project; and it was with still greater uneasiness I saw him persist in his town-scheme, since I am well convinced, that our journey to London must end, like Sir Francis Wronghead's, in a journey into the country again.

I am, Sir,

Your humble servant,

PATIENCE GREENFIELD.

THE GENIUS.

NUMBER X.

Saturday, October 10, 1761.

*Urbem quam dicunt Romam, Melibœe, putavi
Stultus ego huic nostræ similem.*——— VIRG.

Fool that I was, I thought at Rome,
They did the same we do at home;
And by another name, tho' known,
Believ'd that city like our own.

I Have received the following note in consequence of the extract from the Latin Manuscript, with which I presented my readers a few days ago.

To

To the GENIUS.

PLAGUE on your ANEMOLIANS, and non-fenfe, and ftuff! If you have any faults to find with us honeft Britons, why don't you tell us fo in plain Englifh?

Your's.

JOHN TROT.

I am forry to have excited mafter John Trot's indignation; but if his objections to my purfuing the fubject are infuperable, I hereby give him fair warning not to perufe the prefent paper. I fhall only obferve, that travellers, writing chiefly for the inftruction and entertainment of their own countrymen, while they defcribe the manners of foreign nations, and exhibit remote fcenes, are apt, like other fcene-painters, to work *in diftemper*, and draw things and perfons, larger than the life, that they may ftrike at a diftance. This perhaps is in fome meafure, the cafe with our prefent author. The remaining extracts are as follow:

" *Muliere;*

"*Mulieres quidem, &c.* apud M.S.

"THE Anemolian Women are equal in beauty even to the Circaffians, and have alfo learned from fome Europeans, who were caft away on their coaft, the fame method of preferving that beauty from the ravages of the moft cruel of diftempers. This uncommon beauty would give them almoft an abfolute power over the men, if they did not themfelves ufe their utmoft efforts to dim its luftre, and to nip their growing charms in the bud, or to deftroy them in their full bloom: for, as the indelicate females among the Hottentots twine the fat and entrails of animals round their arms and legs, and rub their bodies with filth, thinking thereby to heighten their charms, and render their figures more agreeable; fo the women of Anemolia, not content with that portion of charms which heaven has allotted them, are perpetually retouching by art the beautiful originals of nature, till they become the moft execrable daubs that ever were beheld. If a prince had a palace built of handfome ftone, or perhaps the fineft marble, beautifully variegated by the hand of nature in the quarry, fhould you not efteem him a madman to cover it with plaifter and rough caft?

What

What then shall we say of the women of Anemolia, who pollute the sacred temples of their persons by encrusting them with a coat of Cerufs, and deadening the native vivacity of their features with an artificial enamel? A practice so unnatural has, I find, betrayed me into metaphor and allusion; but the fact, as heaven shall prosper me, is literally true. First, they varnish their faces, necks, and arms, like a whitened wall; and then they lay fantastick colourings, red, brown, or black, according to their various imaginations, upon that ground. Some females have the art of blanching their necks with a curious preparation, which hardens on their bosoms, like mortar in a building; and, like that too, will abide all the changes of the seasons for an whole year. But this process requires time, and confines the lady that submits to it, for some weeks. During the time that I was in ANEMOLIA, I remember it was once the darling piece of scandal among the ladies of quality in NIROE, the capital of that country, that a nobleman's daughter (who, for a few days, ceased to appear at publick places) had absconded, in order to be delivered of an illegitimate child: but the real truth was, thatt he young lady lay in bed a month merely to bring the crust on her neck to a proper confiftency, and bake it, as it were in an oven; and at the end of that period, fhe entirely defeated the malice of her enemies, and confuted their flander, by coming forth with a ghoftly bofom, and as dead a white as alabafter. The greateft misfortune attending this, and every other practife of the like nature, is, that it foon utterly deftroys that exquifite beauty which at firft it ferves but to eclipfe. The mixtures ufed for thefe purpofes are, it feems, compofed of poifon, fo that few retain any of their original charms after they are three or four and twenty years of age; and many of them, even before that period, become horrible to look upon. One of the prevailing beauties at court, at my arrival in ANEMOLIA, was, in a few weeks afterwards, ftruck blind; another object of publick admiration foon after loft all her teeth at once; and a third was fuddenly deprived of the ufe of her limbs, as it were by a ftroke of the palfy, and became bed-ridden. Such dreadful occurrences happened daily, and yet the rifing generation of females continued the practice. This, among many other follies, was originally imported from ACHORIA, where it is not quite fo wonderful that it fhould prevail; for the women of that country, being naturally of a dark and dingy complexion,

complexion, and deftitute of the delicacy peculiar to thofe of ANEMOLIA, more readily recur to the refources of art to mend the imperfection of nature."

I have prefented the reader with the above paffage, becaufe I think it extremely curious; but I cannot help fancying, that our author has tranfgreffed the bounds of credibility in this part of his narrative. It is impoffible that any females fhould be guilty of fuch deteftable wickednefs, or give into fuch grofs abfurdity. The accurate reader will eafily conjecture, from fome peculiarities of expreffion in the above extract, that I have rendered the original with great exactnefs. The tranflation is indeed very literal, except that I have here and there taken the liberty to foften fome phrafes of indignation and reproach which would be efteemed vulgar in our tongue, tho' they have a certain dignity in the learned languages. But to proceed from our M.S.

"The women of Anemolia, confcious of the attraction of their form, and vain of the elegance with which they flatter themfelves they have embellifhed it, are fond of difplaying all its various excellencies. Their arms are uncovered up to the elbow, their necks and bofoms are laid bare, or thinly fhaded with tranfparent veils of the moft delicate

delicate texture. The same vanity induces them to lavish on their persons a profusion of ornaments of gold and silver, and precious stones, and as many ribbands as an heifer of old going to the altar as a sacrifice. They long ago discarded the simple national habit of ANEMOLIA to adopt the fantastick dresses of the ACHORIANS; and so fearful are they of failing to keep pace with that nation in the various changes and revolutions of their garb, that may I perish, if it be not truth!—the cloaths of the chief people in the kingdom, men as well as women, are manufactured and made up in ACHORIA, and transported thence by the first fair wind to ANEMOLIA."

" *Porro autem apud Anemolios meretricum quæstus,* &c. apud M.S.

" Moreover, among the ANEMOLIANS the trade of courtezans, excessive drunkenness, the open exercise of profane swearing, and all manner of gaming, are, undoubtedly, licensed by the laws of the land. I had not time indeed to make a very nice scrutiny into their constitution, and go regularly through the three hundred thousand volumes in which their laws are enrolled; but am nevertheless assured that I cannot be deceived in this circumstance,

circumstance, because the vices above-mentioned are so openly practised, even under the nose of the magistrates, that I am very confident they must have obtained the sanction of publick authority. As soon as the evening comes on, a large number of loose women are ordered to issue forth into the streets, and to use their utmost efforts to decoy passengers into certain houses appointed for their reception. Stated quarters of the metropolis are particularly dedicated to the purposes of riot and debauchery, where lust, drunkenness, and blasphemy, hold their constant reign; while, in other districts of the capital, some of the first dignitaries of the state, principally concerned in the legislature, have instituted societies of gaming : and, indeed, there are few polite families, which have not their meetings of this nature.

" The open practice of so many exorbitant vices, I must confess, created in me much astonishment at my first arrival in the kingdom; but I was, on further reflection, inclined to consider this extraordinary licence, not to say licentiousness, as the effect of deep policy. The promiscuous commerce with loose women is perhaps encouraged in order to turn the minds of the young men from any attempt at adultery, which, it seems, was formerly too
prevalent

prevalent in ANEMOLIA. But the trade of courtezans is not only thus authorized, but the benevolence of the publick has alfo inftituted nurferies for their education, appointed noble provifions for them in their pregnancy, as well as receptacles for their children, and a comfortable retreat for themfelves.—It were alfo to be wifhed, on account of fome fmall inconveniencies at prefent fubfifting, that the courtezans were obliged to wear a numbered ticket, like the porters and hackney coaches among you in England, and made refponfible to certain commiffioners for their behaviour in their profeffion.——Drunkards, and profane fwearers, as well as common beggars, are, I fuppofe, fuffered to infeft the publick ftreets, like the intoxicated flaves which the Lacedæmonians exhibited to their children, in order to deter others from thofe odious practices and fcandalous ways of life: but why every mode of gaming is purfued among them with fo much zeal and vehemence, unlefs it be a part of their religion, I am quite at a lofs to determine or comprehend. On the fame principles with thofe above-mentioned, fuits at law are embarraffed with a thoufand perplexities, prolonged by the moft tedious delays, and loaded with moft heavy expences. The wife caufe of all thefe troubles

troubles attending legal difputes, is, merely to deter the citizens from idle litigations which is evident from their proceedings in matters of a criminal nature. There the offender is brought to an immediate trial, his offence is immedately examined with the utmoft expedition, and the fentence of the law put into immediate execution; upwards of three hundred criminals being publickly hanged every new moon."——I was particularly defirous of laying the above paragraph before the reader, though it contains little elfe than mere matter of reflection, becaufe I think nothing fo much illuftrates a book of voyages, and tends fo much to the improvement of the reader, as the fagacious and juft obfervations with which the traveller is commonly fo kind as to oblige him.——But to proceed from our author.

" *Quod ad Religionem attinet, &c.* apud M.S.

" As to the religion of the country, as I hinted above, I am not able to give a very clear account of it. I was, indeed, in doubt, for fome time, whether the ANEMOLIANS had any fyftem of worfhip eftablifhed among them; but obferving that there was one day, which the commonalty devoted to pleafure and diffolutenefs, I found, upon enquiry,

that

that it was their usual manner of celebrating the sabbath. So far from being destitute of a religion, they may be said to be over run with religions; as a different persuasion prevails in every street, nay, almost in every house. They have many wise teachers, learned in matters of divinity, among their artizans and mechanicks; and there are also several sagacious elderly females who take upon them the care of instructing their own and the other sex in all points of religious faith. Some of them maintain Polytheism, others are given to Deism, and a great number of them are religiously devoted, if I may use the phrase on this occasion, to Atheism. The Europeans, who were thrown on the coast, introduced Christianity among them; but, I am sorry to say it, the true Faith has not taken deep root in ANEMOLIA. Some indeed among them, persons of the purest lives, were struck with the force and dignity of its precepts, and readily embraced the tenets of Christianity: but scoffers at its doctrines soon arose without number; and several authors of the most eminent abilities, and elevated rank, have made it their particular study to write against its doctrines, miracles, &c. though it must be owned, that there

have

have not been wanting full as able advocates on the other fide of the queftion."

" *Vereor hercle ne*, &c. apud M.S.

" I am almoft afraid that what I am now going to relate will hardly obtain credit, as it is fo diametrically oppofite to the courfe of things in every other part of the globe. Few, if any, of the ANEMOLIANS die a natural death. Such as are not put to death by the hands of juftice, or accidents, or fuddenly taken off by apoplexies, palfies, or the like, fall by felf-murder. The rage of fuicide comes on regularly, like the mouiting-time of birds, at a particular feafon of the year, which commences at the fall of the leaf. Mechanicks, and other people of mean condition, commonly hang or drown themfelves; ftatefmen generally die by poifon; and moft of the nobility fall on their fwords, or fhoot themfelves through the head. About the middle of November every pond is filled with carcafes, and dead bodies hang on every tree. I was extremely fhocked at this impious prodigality of their lives; but the furvivors among the natives are not at all affected by it, and behold the daily fuicides, committed by their neareft relations, without the leaft emotion. They told me, that it was conftitutional, either originally in their natures, or generated

generated in them by the climate. They further assured me, that if I remained long among them, the fogs, which are so thick and frequent in that country, would by degrees oppress my spirits, and fill me with a horror of life, and all its attendant vexations.—Other reasons might, indeed, be assigned.—However, I was so shocked and alarmed at this information, that I departed from their country the first opportunity."

The GENIUS.

NUMBER XI.

Thursday, October 29, 1761.

Multa fero, ut placem genus irritabile vatum,
Cum scribo, & supplex populi suffragia capto. Hor.

The spleen of testy authors to subdue,
To bribe the publick voice by flattery too,
An humble author, much I learn to bear,
That when I write, my writings they may spare.

SWIFT, by way of describing a reigning controversy of those times, has left us a most droll and humourous account of a battle of the books in St. James's Library; and Boileau in his
Lutrin

Lutrin has, with equal pleafantry, brought the two adverfe parties in his Poem together in a bookfeller's fhop, where they break out into open war, and convert the books into weapons of offence. Many harmlefs volumes are torn from their fhelves, and fly through the air as thick as hail; and many a French divine lies fprawling beneath the weight of hard-bound poetry, heavy fyftems of philofophy, and huge bodies of the law,

Such a defcription, as that of the French writer, would, I think, be peculiarly applicable to the frequent and violent quarrels among authors. The Republick of letters is in a kind of perpetual civil war, and the beginning of every winter may be confidered as the opening of a new literary campaign. The fhort fummer truce, hardly kept with good faith, is foon violated; and, while heroes fufpend the fhedding of blood in war, authors contend which fhall fpill moft ink in controverfy. One difcharges the blunderbufs of his wit, and out comes an ode: a fecond, after whetting the rufty fword of his Genius, cuts you with a fatire: a third—but it is endlefs to go through all the weapons of elegy, fong, epigram, &c. and recite the whole artillery of wit—to it they go *pêle-mêle*, and, inftead of making a general attack on vice

and

and folly, confine themselves to individual knaves and fools, and fall on one another. It is fortunate enough for all new adventurers in these literary engagements, that they do not make war exactly after the manner described by Boileau; but that every author throws his work, like a bomb, into the town, leaving it to do what mischief it may, without immediately levelling the volume itself at the head of his antagonist. If that were the case, as at the bookseller's in the Lutrin, we have among us many authors, that would be most formidable adversaries even to Homer himself; writers, who could overwhelm all the poets and philosophers of antiquity with a deluge of literature, and carry all before them in a torrent of folios, quartos, and duodecimos, of their own composition.

One would imagine, that every author is a natural enemy to every other author; and that the pursuit of letters, which should refine and humanize the mind, serves only to embitter it. No princes can be more jealous of a neighbour's growing power, than some authors of a cotemporary's infant fame. In their own reputation too they are tender even to soreness, and do not consider, that all, who court applause, may, at the same time, be said to solicit censure. Accordingly,
each

each writer has his flatterers and his enemies; and, if he is vain enough to liften to the adulation of one fet of men, and weak enough to feel the malice of the other, he becomes the moft nnhappy being upon earth. The very nature of his employment betrays him and his quarrels to publick ridicule. Other men differ, and are reconciled in fecret; but the contention of authors is ftudiouſly carried on in the moft open manner, and they cut each other to pieces, like prize-fighters, for the diverfion of the reft of the world.

The great fuccefs of one or two giant fatyrifts, of tranfcendant abilities, has tempted almoft every puny witling to imagine that fame and infamy are at his difpofal. He gives you to underftand, that, unlefs you pay due homage to his extraordinary Genius, your name fhall be regiftered in the black fcroll of difgrace; and he ftands, like a fretful porcupine, ready to dart his quills at all that make him angry. There are, however, a few confiderations, not unworthy the attention of a writer fo fubject to irritability. He may, undoubtedly, be of infinite confequence to himfelf: every man, efpecially every author, is fo: but it is ten to one if he is of equal confequence to the publick: his works indeed, if they are the refult of Genius, may

engage

engage their attention; but his private differences will most probably be thought impertinent. I do not know a more ridiculous circumstance than a couple of scribblers, both big with vanity, calling each other fool and blockhead. It is exactly the scene of Vadius and Trissotin in Moliere; which I am surprised that no one, in this age of authors, has translated for the English stage.—Another reflection,, which might curb their head-strong Pegasus, if he runs riot on the high road of satire, is, that, after all, let him write ever so bitterly, and ever so well, the publick are candid and impartial, and will give him credit no farther than he confirms their own sentiments, and echoes back their own opinion. Pope himself has not been able to rob the eternal butt of his invective, Colley Cibber, of one grain of applause that is due to him; and the united efforts of both him and Swift, powerful as they were, were levelled in vain against Dryden, Vanburgh, Steele, and I will not add Addison. The best answer that an author can make to another who calls him dull (that dreadful sentence!) is to write as well as he can; and if he is not able to confute him that way, he becomes his own satirist. But the chief consideration, which should abate the severity of irritated writers, is,

the

the danger of failing in their attempt. To maim and murder reputations, to hack and hew, and gaſh at random, is, indeed, what any butcherly ſcribbler may attempt; but to keep up the fine edge of true ſatire, requires a very maſterly hand: and if his ſatire proves uncouth, and his execution coarſe, it turns back with ten-fold force upon himſelf, and faſtens on him the odious imputation of malice without wit, and envy without abilities.

But the worſt conſequence flowing from this ill blood between the writers of our times, is, that it diſcourages many men, poſſeſt of noble talents, from exerting them in the cauſe of literature. Fearful of being engaged in this illiberal warfare, they will not venture to commit their pieces to the preſs. They would patiently abide the correction of fair criticiſm, but do not care to provoke unmannerly cenſures.—In this temper of mind the following lines ſeem to have been written: at leaſt, it was the peruſal of them which threw me into the above vein of reflection. Having read them ſeveral times over with pleaſure, I was inclined to try their effect upon my readers, eſpecially as I cannot diſcover in them a line that appears to be *perſonal.*

EPISTLE TO A FRIEND.

"DO, study more—discard that Siren, Ease,
"Whose fatal charms are murd'rous while they
   please.
" Wit's scanty streams will fret their channel dry,
" If learning's spring withhold the fresh supply.
" Turn leaf by leaf gigantick volumes o'er,
" Nor blush to know how antients wrote before.
" Why not, sometimes, regale admiring friends
" With Greek and Latin sprinklings, odds and ends?
" Exert your talents; read, and read to write!
" As Horace says, mix profit with delight."

'Tis rare advice: but I am slow to mend,
Tho' ever thankful to my partial friend:
Full of strange fears—for hopes are banish'd all—
I list' no more to Phœbus' sacred call,
Smit with the Muse, 'tis true, I sought her charms;
But came no champion, clad in cumb'rous arms,
To pull each rival monarch from his throne,
And swear no lady Clio like my own.
All unambitious of superior praise,
My fond amusement ask'd a sprig of bays,
Some little fame for stringing harmless verse,
And e'en that little fame has prov'd a curse;
Hitch'd into rhime, and dragg'd through muddy prose,
By butcher criticks, worth's confed'rate foes.

If then the Muse no more shall strive to please,
Lull'd in the happy lethargy of ease;
If, unadvent'rous, she forbear to sing,
Nor take one thought to plume her ruffled wing;
'Tis that she hates, howe'er by nature vain,
The scurril nonsense of a venal train.
When desp'rate robbers, issuing from the waste,
Make such rude inroads on the land of taste,
Genius grows sick beneath the Gothick rage,
Or seeks her laurels from some worthier age.
   As for Myself, I own the present charge;
Lazy and lounging, I confess at large:
Yet Ease, perhaps, may loose her silken chains,
And the next hour become an hour of pains.
We write, we read, we act, we think, by fits,
And follow all things as the humour hits;
For of all pleasures, which the world can bring,
Variety—O! dear variety's the thing!
Our learned Coke, from whom we scribblers draw
All the wise Dictums of poetick law,
Lays down this truth, from whence my maxim follows,
(See Horace, Ode *Dec. Sext.*—the case Apollo's)
The God of Verse disclaims a plodding wretch,
" Nor keeps his bow for ever on the stretch."

However great my thirst of honest fame,
I bow with rev'rence to each letter'd name;
To worth, where'er it be, with joy submit,
But own no curst monopolies of wit.
Nor think, my friend, if I but rarely quote,
And little reading shines through what I've wrote,
That I bid peace to ev'ry learned shelf,
Because I dare form judgments for myself.
—Oh! were it mine, with happy skill to look
Up to the ONE, the UNIVERSAL BOOK!
Open to all—to him, to me, to you,
—For NATURE's open to the general view—
Then would I scorn the ancients' vaunted store,
And boast my thefts, where they but robb'd before.

Mean while with them, while Græcian sounds impart
Th'eternal passions of the human heart,
Bursting the bonds of ease and lazy rest,
I feel the flame mount active in my breast;
Or when, with joy, I turn the Roman page,
I live, in fancy, in th' AUGUSTAN age!
Till some dull Bavius' or a Mævius' name,
Damn'd by the MUSE to everlasting fame,
Forbids the mind in foreign climes to roam,
And brings me back to our own fools at home.

THE GENIUS.
NUMBER XII.
Thurſday, November 19, 1761.

———Qui vitæ ſervaret munia recto
More; bonus ſane vicinus, amabilis hoſpes,
Comis in uxorem, poſſet qui ignoſcere ſervis,
Et ſigno læſo non inſanire lagenæ. Hor*i*

In ev'ry walk of life his conduct ſcan,
Good Humour, frank and honeſt, marks the man:
Good neighbour, good companion, huſband kind,
And to a ſervant's failings often blind;
Ne'er paying, by a ſottiſh phrenzy led,
A broken bottle with a broken head.

OF all the qualifications of the mind, which are not poſitive virtues, I do not know any that is more deſirable than Good Humour. No quality renders the poſſeſſor more eaſy and happy in himſelf, or recommends him more forcibly to other people. Virtue itſelf receives additional luſtre, abates the rigid ſeverity of its character, and takes its moſt raviſhing graces and embelliſhments from ſuch a diſpoſition; a diſpoſition ſo amiable in its nature, that even a man of loose principles, when of so agreeable a turn, often conciliates to himself many friends and well-wishers. The men at least allow that he is a pleasant fellow, court his company, and account him no-body's enemy but his own; while the women call him a dear agreeable creature, and declare that though, to be sure, he is a wild devil, it is quite impossible to be angry with him.

It is hardly saying too much in favour of this quality, to assert that it is one of the first requisites in society: for though strict honour and integrity are of more essential value in the grand purposes of human life; yet Good Humour, like small money, is of more immediate use in the common commerce of the world. - There is no situation in life, no engagement in business, or party of pleasure, wherein it will not contribute to mitigate disappointments, or heighten enjoyment. A husband, friend, acquaintance, master, or even servant, however faithful or affectionate, will occasion many miserable hours to himself, as well as to those with whom he is connected, if his virtues are not seasoned with Good Humour; and whether he is a partner for life, or a partner in a country-dance, an associate in great and mighty undertakings, or a companion in a post-chaise, he should, on every occafion, cherifh and keep alive this agreeable difpofition.

Some perfons may almoft be faid to be of a good-humoured complexion, and feem to be conftitutionally endued with this amiable turn of mind : a bleffing, for which they may thank heaven with the fame kind of gratitude that he ought to feel, who experiences the comforts of being born in a delightful and temperate climate. My fellow-country-men, I think, are many of them deficient in that airy pleafantnefs, and chearful temper, that diftinguifhes this quality : and as our climate, while it anfwers all the purpofes of ufe and plenty, yet feldom affords us blue fkies, or tempts us to cool grots and purling ftreams, to lie down on the damp grafs, or to thofe other rural delights fo often mentioned by the poets; fo the Englifh themfelves, though overflowing with humanity and benevolence, fuffer clouds of gloomy thoughts to come over their minds, and, however they muft be allowed to be *good-natured*, are feldom remarkable for being *good-humoured*. Yet this half-virtue is worth cultivation, as it beftows new charms on that real one. Good Humour is the fair-weather of the foul, that calms the turbulent gufts of paffion, and diffufes a perpetual gladnefs and ferenity over the heart; and he that finds his temper naturally inclined to break out into sudden bursts of fretfulness and ill-humour, should be as much upon his guard to repress the storm, that is for ever beating in his mind, as to fence against the inclemencies of the season. We are naturally attached even to animals that betray a softness of disposition. We are pleased with the aukward fondness and fidelity of a dog: Montaigne could discover agreeable musick in the good-humoured purring of his cat; and, though our modern grooms and jockies bestow all their attention on make, colour, eyes, and feet, yet the best writers on horsemanship consider a good temper as one of the best qualities in a horse.

We should be the more attentive to encourage and preserve this pleasing quality, because many people lose it by little and little in the progress of their lives. The thoughts of interest frequently proves a growing rust and canker in the mind; and the many troubles and embarrassments attending worldly pursuits often sour the temper, and entirely destroy the spirit of chearfulness and Good Humour that prevailed in the artless and undesigning season of our youth. I do not know a more disagreeable companion, than a man, who,
having

having fet out in life with vaft and vain hopes of advancement, together with a mighty confcioufnefs of his own merit, has not been able to fuftain the fhock of difappointment, but has permitted his misfortunes to embitter his difpofition. Such a man overflows with gall on every occafion, and difcharges the fpleen, that rifes within him, on all his fellow-creatures. He difturbs the peace of the family to which he belongs, and poifons the happinefs of every company to which he is admitted. But the difquiet that he brings with him, whereever he comes, is nothing but an evidence of his own mifery and weaknefs of foul. How much more is he to be imitated, who meets the ftrokes of fortune with an even temper, who fuffers neither reproach nor diftrefs to ruffle his Good Humour, and is, as Hamlet defcribes his friend, " As one, in fuffering all, that fuffers nothing!" Life is like a game at backgammon; and if an unlucky throw comes, we muft make the beft of it, and play on without grumbling at our ill luck: but who would venture to fit down to the table with a man who could not bear an adverfe caft without turning over the board in a fury, and throwing the dice-box at the head of his companion? The character of Sir Thomas More, though peculiarly illuftrious for

unfhaken

unshaken integrity, was in no instance more winning and amiable than in true pleasantry and Good Humour. His chearful behaviour on the scaffold, and in every particular relative to his death, is familiar to all; but there is no circumstance in which the evenness of his mind is more truly delineated, than in his behaviour to his family on his resignation of the Chancellorship. The way in which he discovered it to his wife bespoke the most genuine Good Humour. When he went out of church, it was always usual for some of his officers to go to his lady and acquaint her of his departure: but the Sunday after his resignation, he went himself up to her pew, and, bowing, gravely said, "*Madam, My Lord is gone.*" She, who was accustomed to the facetiousness of his manner, did not immediately comprehend his meaning; but on his explaining the matter to her, as they went home, she began to upbraid him for his shameful inattention to his interest; upon which, without being at all disconcerted by this conjugal lecture, he took occasion to turn the discourse, by finding fault with some part of her dress.—This absolute command of temper, and pleasant vein, is surely to be envied; and he who sees the goods of fortune fall from him, not only without shaking his fortitude, but also

without

without abating the gaiety of his heart, may fairly be said to possess an uncommon share of Good Humour.

SURLY is a man of an easy fortune, humane and benevolent in his nature, and, as Dogberry says, "honest as the skin between his brows;" but he has contracted a kind of habitual peevishness, and every common occasion of life affords him matter of offence. The instant he rises in the morning, he is disquieted with the appearance of the weather, and pours forth execrations on the climate; and when he sits down to breakfast, the water is smoaked, the butter rank, the bread heavy, the news-paper dull and insipid, and his servant sulky or impertinent: yet all the while, he has no malice in his mind, and means no harm to any creature in the world. He has a thousand good qualities, which the quickness of his temper converts into petulance and ill humour. He is a great lover of wit, but cannot bear the least piece of pleasantry on himself; and the most innocent jest touches him to the quick. He will bestow twenty pounds in an act of charity, or do the kindest offices to serve an acquaintance in distress, and the next moment quarrel with his friend for disturbing his reflection by humming an opera-tune. Thus SURLY

Surly lives, much esteemed, and little beloved; and though every body thinks well of him, there are very few that care to cultivate his acquaintance.

But if the want of Good Humour is so conspicuous in a man, of how many charms does it deprive one of the other sex! softness is their distinguishing characteristick; but though, like milk, they are naturally smooth, yet, like milk, they create particular disgust when they turn sour. No female character is more offensive than a Shrew; and the impolite spirit of the English law has provided very rough treatment for termagants, and prepared the severest discipline for the cure of a scold. The greatest reproach on an old maid, that character so much dreaded and ridiculed in the female world, is her ill humour; and crossness is the worst part of a prude. On the contrary, Good Humour, like the Cestus, encircles the fair one with new beauties, and is an antidote to the ravages of age and the small-pox. It is the best part of the portion with a virtuous wife, and a most amiable feature in the face of a Queen.

Among our own sex, there is no race of men more apt to indulge a spirit of acrimony, and to remit their natural Good Humour, than authors. They come abroad, indeed, with a consummate self-
satisfaction

satisfaction and delight; but the least shock given to their vanity taints the mind, and converts all their pleasantry to rancour. The flame of emulation often kindles into envy; and these mettlesome gentlemen press so furiously onward to the goal of fame, that they are sometimes driven to the necessity of jostling one onother in the course. For my part, I would rather chuse to consider myself on a journey than in a race; and surely it is better and pleasanter to jog on in an easy trot, regardless who is left behind, or who is gone before, than to whip and spur a jaded Genius, and, in the heat of furious spleen and blind rage, to be carried perhaps on the wrong side of the post.

Good Humour is the happiest state of mind for a writer, as well as for every other man. Why should an author suffer every hornet of the press to ruffle his temper, or dip his pen in gall, and prepare wormwood draughts to sweeten the ill blood of a cotemporary? He that causelessly and malignantly traduces another, writes a libel on himself; as the highwayman, who makes an attack upon the road, is, in fact, a greater enemy to himself than to the harmless traveller: such a poor wretch, we know, as well as the rest of the gang, will be

brought

brought to juſtice ſooner or later; but no body cares to have their deaths lie at his own door. As for the GENIUS, though he ventures to become a Cenſor, he will never deſcend to the office of Executioner. Even the Muſe of Satire ſhould poſſeſs her graces; and her productions, like the Sweetbrier, ſhould delight and refreſh the ſenſes by their fragrance, while they are armed for our annoyance. If we cannot exerciſe the inſtruments of wit, we can at leaſt lay by the weapons of offence and ill nature; and the candour of the Britiſh Publick will always countenance the fainteſt efforts to railly the reigning vices and foibles of the age with chearfulneſs, pleaſantry, and GOOD HUMOUR.

THE GENIUS.

NUMBER XIII.

Saturday, December 12, 1761.

————————*Corpore in uno*
Frigida pugnabant calidis, bumentia ficcis,
Mollia cum duris, fine pondere habentia pondus.
Hanc Deus et melior litem natura diremit. OVID.

In the fame mafs did hot, cold, moift and dry,
The foft and hard, the light and heavy vie;
Till all thefe jarring elements at ftrife
Nature and Heav'n compos'd, and call'd to life.

TALKING the other evening with a friend, who is fomewhat of a philofophical turn, and loves to deal in abftrufe fpeculations, he fell by degrees into a whimfical vein, and endeavoured to amufe himfelf and me by confidering phyfically, not to fay metaphifically, the probable caufes to which the ftrange diverfities of temper and underftanding among mankind are owing. At one time he fuppofed, that feveral fortuitous circumftances

at

at our birth might produce this variety; and that such an accident as the dilation or compression of the head by the hand of the nurse or the midwife, might determine the infant's future qualities, and mould a hero out of a coward; or squeeze a poet, or a philosopher, into a fool. He had also some conceits about the *Homunculus*, which, however, I shall not presume to explain at present, as a reverend friend of mine, who is deeply versed in those studies, has promised to oblige me with a distinct paper on that subject. He then considered the notions of planetary influence; according to which, all the various actions and dispositions of the human species are governed solely by the stars. On this occasion, he assured me, that an eminent astronomer of his acquaintance was very fatal at casting nativities; and, moreover, that the late revolution in the ministry was absolutely foretold last year in Partridge's Almanack. He dwelt a little on the supposition of the stubborn race of mortals being formed from the stones thrown, as is related by Ovid, over the heads of Deucalion and Pyrrha. From thence he made a quick transition to that kindred Hypothesis, which supposes, that our frames are kneaded out of clay; in pursuance of which, he thought, it was natural to imagine, that the

affections

affections of the mind take their tincture from the veffel in which they are inclofed, and are impregnated, like water, with the qualities of the purer, or bafer earth through which they make their way.

With thefe reflections, the bottle and the coverfation, as is ufual among Englifhmen, ended together, and I retired to my reft. Yet I found it impoffible to fhake off at once the vein of thought which we had been indulging for three or four hours together; and fleep itfelf, inftead of totally difpoffeffing my mind of thofe ideas, rather opened and enlarged my imagination to purfue them ftill further.—The gentle reader is feldom averfe to accompanying the gentle writer in his flumbers; wherefore I fhall venture to relate my dream.

I was fcarce afleep, when I fancied myfelf to be tranfported on a fudden to the verge of the Gulph of Chaos; where, by the tranfient glimmering of an interrupted light, which now and then flafhed upon me, I faw the Four Elements lying in confufion on the boundlefs deep, wherein, as Milton has defcribed it,

—Hot, Cold, Moift, and Dry, Four Champions fierce,
S.rive for the Maft'ry, and to Battle bring
Their embryon Atoms.

I was

I was much affected with the horror of my situation, and expected every moment to be plunged ten thousand fathom deep into the gulph that lay before me, when there emerged from the waves, if I may so call them, of this elemental ocean, a Being of a mild and benevolent aspect, who, after landing on an eminence at some distance, beckoned me towards him with a sort of Caduceus, which he held in his hand, and which was formed in the shape of a Lizard, to signify that he was a friend to Mankind. My fear had deprived me of all power of motion; but the power of his rod drew me insensibly to his side, as it were by a charm. His person was manly and noble: a serene chearfulness was diffused over his countenance: his garment was thrown loosely over him, somewhat after the fashion of a Herald's Coat; and on the four quarters of it were delineated the figures of the Mole, the Whale, the Salamander, and the Camelion, as symbols of the Four Elements, over which, as it appeared, he presided.

My son! saith he, I am the Genius of the Elements. In the vast abyss now before us lie all the future race of Mankind, as it were, in embrio. It is the business of certain spirits, over which I preside, to select from thence the crude materials,

materials, of which all Human Beings are compofed. You, I know, are curious not only to enquire into the various difpofitions of your fellow-creatures, but to inveftigate the caufes, to which their different manners and principles are owing. Thefe caufes I am now going to declare to you; wherefore attend!

Every Mortal is compofed of the Four Elements, but not in equal proportions, nor each mortal in the fame degrees with another. On the contrary, men are, feverally, more or lefs agitated with this or that paffion, or animated with a greater or fmaller proportion of Genius, according to the nature of the particular Element that predominates in their frame; which prevailing Element, whether it be Earth, Water, Air, or Fire, creates the Ruling Paffion, and influences every circumftance of their lives.

In yonder quarter, continued the GENIUS, are formed the fons and daughters of Earth; thofe mortals, I mean, who take their exiftence chiefly from that Element. Thefe are, for the moft part, of a heavy and inanimate difpofition, of groveling fouls and dull minds, and may be rather faid to vegetate than to live. A few, and very few of the Female Sex are compofed of this Element;

and

and thefe are fluttifh in their houfes, flatternly in their perfons, and churlifh to their friends, relations, and hufbands. Thofe of the Male Sex, that owe their origin principally to Earth, are thofe miferly muckworms, who place their fole happinefs in amaffing vaft fums of money; thofe locufts and caterpillars, who eat out the fubftance of others by extortion and ufury. From this Element alfo are fabricated the race of ftupid criticks, and heavy commentators, half-philofophers, entire logicians, dry metaphyficians, and muddling politicians; together with the whole tribe of wretched fcribblers, whom your countrymen have fo properly diftinguifhed by the denomination of Grubs. The particles of which thefe mortals are formed, weigh down their minds, and prevent their foaring to any thing lofty or fublime; for the fame reafon that fathers, according to the principle of that famous chancellor Lord Coke, cannot take an eftate by inheritance from their fons, viz. *becaufe Land*, or Earth, *being of a heavy nature, cannot afcend*. There are, however, among mortals of this terrene compofition, fome who poffefs folid parts and found underftandings; and many, whofe minds are not barren or unfruitful, if they labour to improve them by due cultivation.

Cn

On the banks of that Lake, faid the GENIUS, pointing to another quarter, are created that part of the human fpecies, who draw their life and being from Water. Thefe are commonly found to be cold and phlegmatick in their difpofition; men, who fhelter their native dulnefs and inactivity under the names of caution and prudence; who damp the generous warmth of youth, reprefs the ardour of enterprize, and quench the flame of Genius; women, who can cry when they pleafe; foaking fots, who are for ever moiftening their clay, till they grow maudlin in their liquor, and weep; lovers, who whine away their days in defpair, till at laft they take the Lovers'-Leap into their kindred fea, or drown like blind puppies, in Rofamónd's Pond; tragick authors and actors, who want fire, and draw tears from no eyes but their own: all thefe owe their origin to Water. Among thefe watry fouls, there are indeed fome few, that may be confidered as falutiferous fprings, that are beneficial to their fellow-creatures; or, like noble rivers, which are an ornament, as well as blefling, to the country through which they pafs.

Now, faid the GENIUS, raifing his head, turn your eyes upward, and behold the region from whence they take their being, who are compofed

chiefly

chiefly of Air. These are in general of a light and volatile disposition; often fed with vain hopes, and pleased with empty trifles. Hence are derived the gay race of beaux and fops, who flutter, like butterflies, about the polite world; and in this airy sphere are formed coquettes, jilts, and those females, who are enraptured with romance, or eternally dying with the vapours. Hence descend poets, projectors, and castle-builders without number, who seem to be perpetually endeavouring to climb up to the region from whence they came; and the long train of dependants, who seem to have almost learnt to live, like the Camelion, on their native element, the Air. Hence come the light troop of Essayists, Pamphleteers, Sonneteers, Epigrammatists, &c. whose productions have their beginning in Air, and end in Fire. Of this Element too are composed some daring souls, who take their bold flight, like eagles, and soar to the noblest heights; though never without being followed for a time with a multitude of crows, choughs, and ravens, who pursue them with hoarse and dissonant cawings, and disturb earth and heaven with their clamour.

Lastly, continued the GENIUS, behold the bright district where those mortals are formed, who are composed principally of Fire. These are, for the most

most part, of a warm and paſſionate nature; amongſt whom the virtues and vices are to be found in their extremes. Here too you may find men of hot heads, and ladies of warm conſtitutions. Hence comes the termagant, who is all rage and fury, and the hero, who is all glory and gunpowder. Hence alſo comes the ſpirited race of bucks, bloods, libertines, and freethinkers. Hence too are derived many of thoſe glorious and ſublime ſages, heroes, princes, poets, and philoſophers, whoſe Genius throws a luſtre all around them, and who ſeem to be placed, like beacons, amidſt the human ſpecies, to hold forth lights to the reſt of the world.

Happy, ſaid the GENIUS, is he, who has learnt to temper the irregularities of his frame, ſo as to prevent the evil effects of the Element that prevails in his compoſition! Happier ſtill is that man, in whom the Elements are mixed in the neareſt proportion to each other.

At theſe words, whether from ſudden noiſe, ſufficient reſt, a deſire to reply, or from what other cauſe I know not——I awoke.

THE GENIUS.

NUMBER XIV.

Thursday, December 31, 1762.

Vester, Camænæ, vester in arduos
Tollor Sabinos: Seu mihi frigidum
Prænefte, seu Tibur supinum,
Seu liquidæ placuere BAIÆ. HOR.

Sweet Muses, yours', all yours' in town,
Yours' to the Country, I go down;
Whither Thames, Dee, or rocky Tweed,
Or BATH's warm Springs my fancy lead.

BATH, and Tunbridge, and Cheltenham, and Scarborough, and the other Watering Places of this kingdom, although many miles distant from the metropolis, and some of them scarce to be brought within the compass of a day's journey, even in this age of expedition, when

the

the flying waggon is no extraordinary *Phænomenon*, may yet be juftly confidered as places of publick diverfion belonging to the town. The Rooms in no wife refemble other country affemblies, where the fquire commands refpect, and derives additional authority from being in the commiffion of the peace; and the balls are quite in a different ftile from a dance at the affizes, where the aldermens' wives and daughters fet off with the neweft patterns, from London, are admitted to drop a curtfy to the ladies of the reprefentatives for the town or country, or, perhaps, even to the Lady Lieutenant. On the contrary, the company of thefe places make up the fame fantaftical medley, nay, confifts of the very fame perfons as occafionally compofe the groupe in the places of entertainment in and about London; and while we are fure to encounter the well-known faces that haunt every houfe and garden whofe doors are thrown open to receive them, notwithftanding the 'real diftance, we can fcarce fuppofe ourfelves beyond the limits of the bills of mortality, any more than we are apt to fancy ourfelves out of town, when we have juft got off the ftones towards Vauxhall or Ranelagh.

In

In this light, at least, I was tempted to consider this matter in a late trip to Bath—with this only difference: in town, the company is brought together for a few hours only; and though some may have repaired thither on foot, some in equipages decorated with bloody hands and coronets, and others in coaches distinguished by square plates of painted tin, yet, on their separation, who can tell what becomes of his late associates, any more than where they came from? At Bath, and the like places, each person may be said not only to exhibit himself for a time, but even to live in publick. He resides in a house of glass, and all his words, actions, pleasures, and attachments, are known to the whole circle of the little world he inhabits. Neither my lord, nor my lady, who disdain to sin in private, nor the petty trespasser, who loves to be snug in his offences, are exempt from observation. Almost every body descants on the characters of others, and almost every body exposes his own. It is a kind of general *bob* or *nob*, or give and take, as Shakespeare explains the phrase, between all the good company. The old, the young, the rich, the poor, the sick, the well, English, French, Germans, Swifs, and Italians, all live here together, as it were, in one family; and with as little emotion of mutual concern or regard, as thofe who are really of one family, commonly have for each other.

Bath no more owes its entire fupport to mere invalids, than the univerfities are filled with real ftudents; or than the Temple coffee houfes are totally maintained by lawyers that have bufinefs, or Child's and Batfon's by phyficians that have practice. If every faunterer in the Pump-Room was to be ftrictly interrogated concerning the motive of his coming thither, or the manner of his paffing his time there, diffipation, play, and intrigue, would appear to have drawn after them a larger retinue than the gout or the cholick. A perfon, who is fond of taking an eftimate of manners and principles, might find here much matter, of fpeculation. For my own part, being too poor to game, too well to drink the waters, too dull, or too brifk, too wife, or too foolifh, too infenfible, or too what you will, to fall in love, I remained an idle fpectator of the bufy fcene before me; and like a dull geographer, without pretending to account for the nature of the foil, or to difcover the feveral fprings and mines that lay underneath, I contented myfelf with taking a curfory furvey of the place, and

and drawing out a map from what appeared on the face of the country.

It affords abundant matter of congratulation to this kingdom, that notorious games of hazard, such as the E. O. Tables, and the like, are at length banished from these places, as well as from the masquerade and ridotto. There are still, it is true, to be found several hungry cormorants, eager to feed on the ignorant or unwary; and studious to make use of the opportunities arising from the promiscuous mixture of the cheat and the dupe, the gentleman and the sharper. They, however, who are weak enough to fall a prey to these sharks of society, are the less to be pitied, as they seem to devote themselves to destruction with their eyes open. The characters of these vagrant gamblers are generally notorious. He, therefore, who ventures his hundreds against the last stake of a fellow, whom he would not admit into his house, or speak to, but across the card-table, surely suffers himself to be robbed, while he feels the hand of the cut-purse in his pocket; and has no more right to complain of ill treatment, than if he had descended to play with link-boys, and pick pockets in a night cellar.

Far

Far be it from me to endeavour, with rude hand, to force open the cabinet of love, or to unlock the secrets of the Temple of Cupid ! Love, however determined on secrecy, is apt to break out and betray itself unawares, to make itself known by a thousand little inadvertencies and absurdities in our conduct, the involuntrary emotions of tenderness. Rather, therefore, would I admonish these sweet triflers, in the supposed words of Cassio to Desdemona, "*let us be wary! let us hide our loves!*" in order to which, let them abstain from billing and cooing in publick, from rolling of eyes, and squeezing of hands, and joining of knees under the table! Idleness and curiosity are ever on the watch; and Scandal, like Virgil's Fame, has as many eyes as tongues. It is a maxim at Bath, and all other publick places, that when a young couple have been partners at a ball for two nights together, every other point is settled between them; whereon the banns of marriage are published in the Rooms, long before the time for their declaration any where else. Making love may be, and no doubt is, a very engaging entertainment to the parties concerned; but there is no scene of courtship, which does not appear exttemely ridiculous in the eyes of an indifferent spectator.

But

But if the sparks of honourable love are, in these common haunts of men, to be thus cautiously repressed from bursting into a blaze, what shall we say to the unwarrantable ebullitions of the spirit of intrigue? If a fine lady, just broke loose from her husband, or a warm widow lately relieved from the yoke of matrimony, have a mind to give their passions full play, why need they advertise their intentions to the whole world? Or, if a sprightly young fellow has subdued some frail piece of female virtue, is it not cruel to make his conquest publick? In a word, why should both parties prefer an open scorn of virtue and decorum to the concealment of their vices? It would be too rigid and unreasonable to debar persons of spirit entirely from their pleasures. I would only advise them to be temperate and discreet in the use of them. The cuckoldly husband might put his horns quietly into his pocket, if he was not industriously pointed out for a monster; and the world might wink hard at female frailties, if they did not provoke attention, and peremptorily challenge observation. Open gallantries are sure to become the subject of town-talk; and the rumour of Bath and Tunbridge intrigues is as quickly calculated through the

best

best company, as a box on the ear indiscreetly dealt at Ranelagh.

There is no part of these mixt assemblies, which I am apt to consider with more compassion, than those unfortunate young females, whose wise relations are fond of carrying them to and fro, from one publick place to another, by way of introducing them early to the knowledge of the world, or as the means of getting them a husband. There is, indeed, no situation, where a decent and amiable behaviour in a young lady would be more conspicuous: but those, who have been formed on the above-mentioned system of education, have commonly lost all their domestick graces, without having acquired any allurements in exchange for them. They know the rules and customs of publick places, without being in the least acquainted with the manners of the world, which are not to be collected in a giddy life of perpetual dissipation, or learnt with the graces of a minuet, and the figure of a country dance, or picked up by chance at the lottery table; as a proof of which, it seldom happens, that these female pupils of *Flirtation* contract an advantageous match, though they often fall a prey to the professed rake or libertine. Or, if that is not the case, they are hawked about from place to place, till *the bloom is off the plum*, when, (to purſue the alluſion) many nauſeate the fruit, ſo ſoon is grown dead and ſtale in the market, which perhaps they would have gathered with pleaſure, if it had been left to hang its due time upon the tree.

If there are any characters of this motley drama that move our mirthful indignation more powerfully than all the others, it is the ſwarm of humble retainers to the Great, that are for ever buzzing in the ear of nobility. The eaſy intercourſe between perſons of different ranks, which this place affords, is particularly grateful to theſe *ſpunges*, as Hamlet terms them, who delight to ſoak up the countenances of people of faſhion. This numerous tribe is made up of both ſexes; and happy is he or ſhe who can be occaſionally called in to fill up a vacant corner in her Grace's party at Quadrille; and how woeful is the mortification, if they ſhould fail to edge themſelves into his Lordſhip's tea-drinking! Such ſelf-made dependants, who are engendered by the ſmiles of the Great, like flies or maggots out of carrion by the rays of the ſun, have no idea of any diſtinction between perſons, except that which title beſtows on them. They ſeem indeed to ſuppoſe themſelves

noble

noble and genteel by reflection, though they fink in the estimation of others, in proportion as they rise in their own. They are considereed in general as runners to the great, that fetch and carry, come and go, as they are bid. Though they flatter themselves that they mix in the polite world, they live but in the suburbs and out-skirts of gentility. They are, in truth, but a mean appendage to the great, a higher, but yet more infamous degree, of pages and lacquies to hold up the tail of nobility, or rather a contemptible part of the train itself; a narrow edging or border, a kind of beggar's tape that binds the hem of quality.

The late and ever-memorable Richard Nash, Esq. whose name is almost as much revered at Bath, as that of the great Bladud himself, for some few years before his death published proposals for printing, by subscription, The History of BATH and TUNBRIDGE. Many, who subscribed largely to this work, contrary to the case of all other subscriptions, would have been much disappointed and offended, if it had ever made its appearance; so that the price of subscription might be considered as hush-money, to keep the intrigues and gallantries of the nobility in silence. The original papers, containing many curious anecdotes, are

fallen

fallen into my hands; and, unless the dukes and dutchesses, peers and peeresses, in general, and others the gentry of this realm, will subscribe their *five guineas* to me, The GENIUS, as nobly as they did to the first author, the work shall certainly come out. In the mean time, the manuscripts are lodged in the hands of an eminent counsel, as it is said was the case with some of Pope's Epistles and Satires, that we may be enabled to go just upon the edge of libel and *scandalum magnatum*. Those who would not have their adventures and amours recorded in this secret history, may take the gentle hint I now give them, and send in their subscriptions to the printer of this paper. In the mean time, I would recommend it to Messrs. Wiltshire and Simson at Bath, as well as to the proprietors of the pump-room, and masters of the coffee-houses, to hang the rooms with the ST. JAMES's CHRONICLE.

THE GENIUS.
NUMBER XV.

Saturday, January 9, 1762.

―――――――*Ubi quid datur oti,*
Illudo chartis. ――――――― Hor.

When I've nothing elfe to do
I play at Whift, Quadrille, or Lu.

ON my return home a few evenings ago, I found lying on my table a foiled knave of diamonds, bearing evident marks of having ferved in feveral campaigns, which I found, on examination, to come from my old acquaintance, Mrs. Marrcourt, and to contain an invitation, written in her own old Englifh black letter, to a private party at cards, on Monday the fourth of January.

Mrs. Marrcourt is the widow of a gentleman who had a place in the houfehold, and at her hufband's death obtained, by the intereft and follicitation of fome powerful friends, an annual penfion of a hundred and fifty pounds. Having had, as she often says herself, a very genteel education, and always lived in a polite sphere, she entertains the most profound respect for all persons of fashion, as well as an implicit veneration for all the manners, appurtenances, and dependences, of quality. Wherefore, notwithstanding the narrowness of her income, she never could endure the thoughts of being exiled from the great world, but has been reduced to several shifts to maintain the appearance of a tolerable footing in it. Being now grown aged and infirm, she cannot well crawl through the park in fair weather, or along the best paved streets to pay her morning visits. She is, however, in possession of the cast sedan of a countess of her acquaintance, by whom she was honoured with it as a present seven years ago; but being unable to pay her chairmen the usual rates for weekly attendance, she drives a hard bargain, and retains them at an under price; whence it often happens, that her two chairmen are not only in liveries of two different colours, but she is obliged to be carried by all the raw-boned, unpractised fellows, who jumble along in a rough trot, as uneasy as a stage-coach over the stones; and no sooner have they learnt to pace along in the true human amble, and

become

become capable of better bufinefs, than they defert the good old lady, and their places are fupplied by a frefh pair of hackney novices; fo that fhe has the breaking-in of moft of the two-legged colts in town. She has apartments in one of the old palaces, *gratis*; and during the fummer-months, becaufe fhe would not, for the world, be fo ungenteel as to ftay in London, fhe takes a two-penny lodging at Greenwich or Richmond. She conftantly vifits at feveral great houfes, and though often fhut out, by perfeverance and the utmoft good-breeding, fhe is fometimes let in, and perhaps, if there is no particular company, afked to ftay dinner. The ladies treat her with a haughty familiarity, and ftile her plain Marrcourt: and the facetious men of fafhion make mock love to her, compliment her, in the ftrain of well-bred raillery, on her perfon, beauty, tafte, and other qualifications; freely indulging themfelves in all thofe liberties, which young fellows, con-fcious and vain of their rank, are apt to take with their inferiors.—Yet, even from this kind of con-nection with people of diftinction, does Mrs. Marr-court derive no fmall degree of confequence. She remembers the day fhe bought her laft pound of tea, by recollecting it was the fame on which fhe dined

dined at his lordship's; she talks familiarly of Lady Harriot and Lady Mary; and is reckoned, by all the lower gentry of her acquaintance, to be *a mighty genteel sort of body, and to keep none but the very best of company,*

I waited on Mrs. Marrcourt on the evening appointed, but perceived, immediately on my entrance into her apartments, that although she had given her assembly the modest appellation of a private party, she had in fact collected all the company she was able, with a particular view to bring together some persons of rank and dignity. Her two rooms, the largest of which is scarce bigger than a cabin, and the least a mere closet, were so crouded, that it was with the utmost difficulty that I could squeeze my little person sideways between the backs of the chairs belonging to the several card tables, in order to make my way from one end of the place to the other. The tables were, many of them, placed diagonally, by which means she had been able to edge in one or two extraordinary; and most of the company, who were not put down to cards, stood in a huddle by the fire-side, and the remaining few had disposed themselves in the seats of the windows. The room was lighted up with the ends of wax-candles,

bought

bought of the duke of ——'s butler, and the company regaled with a small liquor, made by Mrs. Marrcourt herself, in the present scarcity of lemons, of the best Cream o' Tartar. The company itself was as miscellaneous as a pack of cards, or any hand that can be formed from different combinations of them; but the most distinguished members of it, and to which I observed Mrs. Marrcourt paid particular attention, were, an old Irish peer, of a disputed title, a Creolian colonel, a distressed baronet, a city knight and his lady, a French gentlewoman from the neighbourhood of Soho, an old general officer on half-pay, and a yellow admiral.

Such is the faithful picture of the good old lady's assembly; and without pretending to more than ordinary penetration, we may venture to pronounce that there are many Mrs. Marrcourts in this great metropolis. Nor is it any matter of surprise; for if ladies of distinction will delight to throw open their great gates, and court the whole tide of nobility to flow in upon them, there will ever exist these minor dames of second-hand gentry, fond of aping the vices and follies of their superiors. But though the imitation of bad things, like the corruption of the best, renders them most odious and contemptible,

contemptible, it may not be amiss to carry our reflections still further, and to consider the nature of the politest of these assemblies, set off with every circumstance of elegance and splendor.

These genteel meetings, like Milton's Pandæmonium, *frequent and full*, are, in the dialect of the fashionable world, denominated Routs; the signification of which word, according to dictionaries of the best authority, is as follows. Johnson defines a Rout to be *a clamorous multitude; a rabble; a tumultuous croud:* and Giles Jacob, in his Law Dictionary, declares the word ROUT to signify an Assembly *of persons, gathered together, and going to execute, or indeed executing, an unlawful act*. If we examine the thing itself as it appears in high life, we shall be convinced of the propriety of the term, and cannot but allow that all these Routs, from that of a dutchess down to Mrs. Marrcourt's, come within the meaning of both these descriptions. For what is a Rout but a *tumultuous croud; a rabble;* that is, a genteel mob, or the rabble of quality, *drawn together,* as Jacob says, *and going to execute, or indeed executing, an unlawful act?*

But the prevailing idea is, undoubtedly, the Croud; and the lady, who is mistress of the Rout, is

is happy in proportion to the numbers fhe has been able to affemble. If the publick way is interrupted for three ftreets together, and the company can fcarce get to and fro between the houfe and their coaches and chairs; if the boxes at the play or the opera are robbed of their company, becaufe thofe, who are left uninvited, are afhamed to betray the contempt or neglect they are doomed to fuftain; if in the moft fpacious apartments in London, the company are crouded together, as clofe as at Mrs. Marrcourt's, or as the poor prifoners in the black-hole at Calcutta; the triumph is more ample and complete. I remember a dutchefs and a countefs, who for a time entertained the moft mortal averfion for each other, from having both appointed their Routs on the fame day of the week. The whole town, at leaft the polite part of it, was divided into parties; and ranking themfelves, as under a banner, beneath the colours of the cards, were feverally called the Reds and the Blacks. The parties being equally powerful, and the Routs of each being of courfe rendered lefs numerous, who can fay to what extremities matters might have been carried, if a man of fafhion, who, like a blank card, had yet received no impreffion either from Red or Black, had not
fortunately

fortunately compromised the affair, and prevailed on the ladies to be content with taking the day alternately, each holding a Rout only once in a fortnight?

It is remarkable, that this rage for a Croud has produced a most extraordinary revolution in dress. A friend of mine has composed a most elaborate treatise, in the manner of Montesquieu, on the causes of the rise and fall of the hoop-petticoat. In the learned section on the subject of ROUTS, which is as curious as any chapter in Tristram Shandy, the author has plainly demonstrated, that these assemblies have produced a total revolution in architecture and dress. Every house is built as if it was intended to receive the whole town; and every lady is drest as if she was going into apartments where she would not have room to turn herself round. The hoop, which had stood the shocks of ridicule for forty years together, which dilated itself wider and wider on every new attack, which incumbered whole apartments, spread itself all over the Mall, eclipsed beaux, and overshadowed side-boxes, shrunk in an instant, like a flower shut up at sunset, or a closed umbrella. *No Hoops* became the common *Nota Bene* to all cards of invitation; and the ladies came abroad, suddenly

suddenly freed of all their tumours and incumbrances, like a new mother juft delivered of her burthen, or like the fallen angels in Milton, as on a fignal given,

> ———————— to fmalleft Forms
> Reduced their Shapes immenfe; and were at large,
> Though without Number ftill.

It may almoft be afferted, without a quibble, that the fyftem of life, now eftablifhed in the polite world, feems calculated to deftroy fociety for the fake of company. A Lady's Journal is a mere calendar of vifits and routs; vifits often paid by the footmen, with a flip of card and a flambeau; and Routs, where, inftead of a few felect friends, fhe meets with a croud of half acquaintance and ftrangers. ROUTS are the modern fchools of education for the female fex; and as cards feem to be deftined for their fole amufement and employment, I would advife my good friend Mr. Newberry, the annual publifher of the Ladies Memorandum Book, to difpofe his next into the popular form of a pack of cards, the two and fifty cards, of which the pack confifts, naturally adapting themfelves to the ufe of the two and fifty weeks, into which the year is diftributed. The

feveral

several Sundays might be distinguished as the first, second, third, or fourth Sundays of the dutchess of A's, the countess of B's, lady Van D's, or Mrs. E's Rout; and the little spaces allotted for appointments, might be filled with secret assignations, if it be true, (as the Chronicle of Scandal relates) that such assignations are sometimes made at these assemblies.

I have been the more earnest to throw together my reflections on this subject at present, because the female passion for ROUTS grows every day more and more predominant, and I am credibly informed that the contagion has actually spread even to our colonies, and been carried by our country-women into other parts of the world. General Assemblies, of no parliamentary nature, I am told, are frequently held in New England; the clerks of our East-India Company and their wives have, it is said, been known to lose a lack of rupees at a sitting at Bengal; and I am confidently assured, that a lady of quality, on her travels, has so far broke in upon the simplicity of the Cantons, as to have absolutely established an evening assembly for halfpenny Lu in Switzerland.

In order, therefore, to prevent the further evil consequences resulting from these private publick gaming-

gaming-houses, and at the same time not entirely to deprive persons of distinction of their favourite amusement, and yet to render it of some small utility and advantage, I would humbly submit to the attention of the legislature the following plan of a ROUT-ACT. No lady, of whatsoever rank, should be allowed to hold in one night more than three card-tables for Whist, Cribbage, or Quadrille; which, with a fourth for the use of the more promiscuous games, such as Lansquenet, Lu, Lottery, &c. may fairly be supposed to comprehend all the persons that can meet at once for the sake of society. But, for the entertainment of those, who delight in larger assemblies, two publick ROUTS should be instituted, with authority to open their doors every night, like the theatres: one to be held, for the use of the court end of the town, at Carlisle House, Soho Square; and the other, for the ladies of the merchants, aldermen, and common-council men, at Haberdasher's-Hall in the city. The card-money, as well as the sums subscribed for admission, (instead of being lavished on butlers, *valets*, and *maitres d'hotel*) should be laid apart, in order to create a fund for the support of decayed gamesters, whose necessities might be supplied by their successors at the gaming-table, as the stage

now

now and then gives a benefit for diftreft and fuperannuated actors. By thefe means a lord, who has exhaufted his fortune by deep play, need not degrade himfelf by application for a penfion; and a merchant who has, by the like conduct, involved himfelf and family in the miferies of bankruptcy, need not do the world and his creditors a further injury by going into bufinefs again.

END OF THE GENIUS,

ORIGINALLY PUBLISHED IN

THE ST. JAMES's CHRONICLE.

THE

GENTLEMAN,

ORIGINALLY PUBLISHED IN

The LONDON PACKET.

THE GENTLEMAN.

NUMBER I.

Friday, July 10, 1775.

Fac periclum in literis,
Fac in palæstrâ, in muficis: quæ liberum
Scire æquum est, folertem dabo.　　TER.

Try him in Letters, Exercifes, Mufick!
In all the Arts A GENTLEMAN fhou'd know,
I'll warrant him accomplifh'd.　　COLMAN'S TERENCE.

OF all bodies of men, Authors may juftly claim the largeft fhare of publick fpirit. Strenuous advocates for the rights of the people, they have not only even fhewn themfelves vigilant guardians of the liberty of the prefs, but have alfo recently manifefted a noble contempt for what appeared to be their own more immediate concern,

VOL. I,　　　M　　　　　*the*

the property of the press; a property which they have lately seen voted away with a true stoical apathy and indifference. They have silently beheld, like unconcerned spectators, its very existence denied, and have acquiesced in the sublime doctrine of disinterestedness to the greatest extreme. Physicians and lawyers avowedly plead and prescribe for a fee, soldiers fight for pay, and even divines preach and pray for a benefice. The labourer, in other stations, is reckoned worthy of his hire. Authors alone are content to have little other recompense than fame for their labours, and quietly allow that a general *imprimatur* converts their works into general property. The industrious commonwealth of literature has been plundered of the wax and honey, without one of the exhaustless hive endeavouring to fix his sting into his spoilers: but in vindication of the *liberty* of the press, not a drone but would join in instant commotion.

The Liberty of the Press is indeed a most glorious privilege. When it is but mentioned every Englishman swells with a conscious superiority, and seems to feel himself half an inch taller; if on the Continent, the thought almost adds a cubit to his stature; yet this liberty, invaluable as it is, like all other liberty, has been shamefully abused; and has
oftentimes

oftentimes been exercifed with the barbarity of favages, rather than the gallant fpirit of freemen; by monfters wielding the pen, not as the fword of publick juftice or defence, but ufing it as the inftrument of ruffian violence and private rancour. In political difcuffions, indeed, freedom of fentiment and fpeech fhould be almoft boundlefs: and a great and enterprifing genius, beft able to go all lengths, might perhaps with great propriety try, " how far the Liberty of the Prefs could legally be carried:" but in writings of a private nature, that doctrine becomes fhameful and fcandalous, and the practice almoft diabolical. He who exercifes the Liberty of the Prefs, with no farther idea of reftraint, than what the law impofes, may efcape a partial profecution, but will incur univerfal contempt: for the rogue within the law, as any attorney can teftify, is the moft dangerous and defpicable of all rogues. In a moral as well as a civil fenfe, every man's houfe fhould in fome meafure be his caftle; and the mifcreant who wantonly difturbs the repofe, or breaks into the harmlefs fecrets, of a private family, commits a kind of literary burglary, and is almoft as culpable as the minifter or king's meffenger who fhould now attempt the *feifure of papers,* or dare to enter a manfion by a

General Warrant. The English are a remarkably good-natured, as well as generous people; but were a stranger to form a character of them from a perusal of their daily publications, they would appear to require a constant evening sacrifice to their ill-nature, and a hecatomb of reputations for their breakfast.

Seeing the colour of many other publications, and those, alas, too generally popular, I mean occasionally to hazard an essay in this paper, of a complection totally different, and now and then to rescue at least one column, in one news-paper, from scandal and politicks. The recess of parliament, when the minds of men are less heated by contention, is a proper season to commence such an undertaking. For my own part, I am at present writing inclined to trust the interests of my country, on both sides of the Atlantick, to the three great branches of the legislature; but if I find them inadequate or unfaithful, I shall be happy with other authors to *embody*, like the constitutional militia, in times of danger, and to change *the Gentleman* into *the Politician*, as Steele converted *the Guardian* into *the Englishman*. Even Quakers perhaps might, on such an occasion, suspend the pacifick tenets of their persuasion; and even some of our Clergy

would,

would, in such circumstances, exhibit a new idea of Church Militant, change their gowns for coats of mail, and like a boiled lobster, turn from black to red.

It is however at present my wish and my intention to suffer my patriotick powers of writing to sleep, like the sword in the scabbard. Every Gentleman chuses to wear one both for ornament and defence, but when he puts it on, says to himself with Mercutio, " Heaven send me no need of thee!" I will not, like the court-fool of old times, run a muck against the King and his Nobles; I will not draw my wit upon the Minister; much less (as I have already professed) will I wound the bosom of domestick tranquillity. I send these fugitive papers smiling into the world, wishing them, like Swedes' Tea, to sweaten the blood and juices of my Countrymen, and to correct their ill humours; but tho' intended for an antidote to black bile and acrimony, it is hoped they will not appear, like Magnesia, a cure for the heart-burn indeed, but in themselves a drug tastelefs and insipid. The rose and sweet-briar are not the less fragrant for the thorn that makes a part of them; and the powers of satire and ridicule, while pointed at general vices and enormities, are not only innocent but

but falutary. Bungling quacks cannot attack the difeafe, without injuring or perhaps killing the patient: but the true moralift fees the drama of fociety performed before him, like the fkilful naturalift contemplating bees through a glafs hive, marking their operations, and turning them to account, without offering the bufy infects the leaft injury. The prefent age fwarms with follies, and teems with characters worthy of obfervation. Such will be frequently exhibited; but as they are intended, like thofe of the New Comedy of Menander, to be general, it is hoped that none of them will be challenged by any individual.

The Motto prefixed to this Indroductory Effay may perhaps be thought arrogant; but it is only meant to imply fuch fubjects as are fit for difcuffion on a plan of this liberal nature, and fuch a character as the writer would wifh to exhibit in the perfon of The Gentleman: not that he prefumes to hint that he fhall himfelf be found equal to it. He means to derive his chief importance from the merits of others. As to himfelf, whether really a Gentleman, or the meaneft Plebeian; a ftudent at his eafe, or a fcribbler in the Fleet; fitting by a filver ftandifh in his own apartment, or with a broken ink-bottle in a garret or cellar; are matters

of

of no importance to the reader, so long as the author shall sustain the part he has assumed. Though appearing in a publick character, he means to be namelefs and unknown. He has drawn up the curtain, like other managers, without admittance behind the scenes, an indulgence which might gratify the curiosity of a few, but tends to destroy the publick entertainment. In his bills the director can at present announce no more than *The Gentleman*, to which the wags (if they please) may subjoin, *being the first time of his appearing in that character*. I must beg leave, however, once for all to declare, that with whatever notice they may honour me, to their wit or their dulness I shall never make any reply; not from the spirit of silent contempt, but rather on the principle of Fielding, who when he was told in the Green Room that the audience were damning his Comedy, acquiesced in the badness of it, and cried, *What! have they found it out!*

It has been suggested to me, that it would be more consonant to the character of a Gentleman, to send forth my speculations, like some of my predecessors, uncontaminated by paragraphs and advertisements, beautifully printed on a sheet and half of fine writing paper: but many of my superiors,

superiors, several excellent essayists, moral and political, have written in news-papers. As to that, in which The Gentleman has chosen to insert his Productions, he has distinguished it on a principle of publick spirit; having observed it for some time past to have been the deadest, dullest, most unentertaining and insipid of the many Journals and Chronicles which the press groans under at present; a circumstance the more extraordinary, as it is, he is informed, the property of a junto of the sprightliest, wittiest, politest, and most learned spirits of the age; capable of instructing and enlivening it with every species of composition, from History down to a Pun or an Epigram. The very Printer, Mr. William Woodfall, if Fame say true, is able, like the silkworm, to weave his own rich materials, and, after the example of the Stevens's and Elzevirs, to be himself the editor of any productions that might issue from his press. To stimulate therefore these capable but indolent geniusses, to rouse them from their lethargy, to set all hands to work on board the London Pacquet, is the design and ambition of *The Gentleman*; happy, if like Falstaff, he should at any time be found to be witty himself, but content if he can at least, like Falstaff, be the cause of wit in other men.

THE GENTLEMAN.

NUMBER II.

Wednefday, July 12, 1775.

Alterius fic
Altera pofcit opem res, & conjurat amicè. Hor.

Allied, as fifter clofe to brother,
One thing ftill afks the help of t'other;
And thus allied, both He, or She,
From love, or int'reft, will agree.

IT is ufual with thofe who exhibit their performances to the Publick, to follow up their firft effort with an account of the great and uncommon applaufe that has been beftowed on it. As I have always imagined fuch accounts to be religioufly true, I cannot help confidering myfelf as deplorably unpopular, or peculiarly unfortunate. I have not heard a fyllable uttered in favour of the firft Number of The Gentleman, and almoft all the readers I expected to intereft or engage, have been occupied with the Seffions Paper or the London

London Gazette. I have not seen a single copy of verses in praise of my style, and I have even been assured by my friends, that the people of this country will not at present read any article in a newspaper longer than a paragraph. I have however been honoured with the notice of *two* correspondents; and as they seem inclined, on certain conditions, to become assistants in my present undertaking, I shall introduce them to my readers by making their Letters publick, before I proceed in my own speculations.

To the Author of The GENTLEMAN.

"SIR,

"I HAVE the honour to be a BLACKGUARD, and if it had not been for a few touches in your paper, that shewed you to be no enemy to Vulgar Manners, as well as no mean proficient in the Vulgar Tongue, I should have beheld your Essays with silent contempt, and would not have condescended to correspond with you. But is this a time, Sir, for a writer who means to amend the morals, or correct the behaviour, of the idle things, and puppies of the present age, to usher a work into the world under the title of *The Gentleman?* Do not false
refinements,

refinements, affected politenefs, and in a word, *Gentility* (as they term it) threaten to undermine our morals, pervert our good fenfe, and infect our behaviour? Formerly it was the boaft of this country, that every man might, in things indifferent, vary from his neighbour. Private Liberty was as effential a mark of our manners, as Publick Liberty was the characteriftick of our conftitution: no principles of politenefs, no fyftem of behaviour, no rules for raifing a French or Italian fuperftructure on a Gothick foundation, but every man built his reputation on the bafis of good fenfe and good nature. At prefent we begin to refine, and file, and polifh, 'till our manners, as Sterne faid of thofe of our neighbours, are growing as fmooth and undiftinguifhable as an old King William's halfpenny; and fafhionable principles, like the legs of fafhionable furniture, have fcarce ftrength enough to fupport the frame that belongs to them.

"*Gentility*, Sir, (give me leave to repeat and infift on it) is the great bane of our lives, the nurfe of vice, diffipation and extravagance; the parent of bankruptcy, and fource of corruption. Foreign manners will not thrive under our meridian. There is a kind of *Magna Charta* in our good fellowfhip, fellowship, as well as in our laws, that will not brook the controul of an honest hearty laugh, or endure to be fettered by Dissertations on Left Legs.

" In opposition to the contemptible animal, the new-fangled being, that now commonly distinguishes itself by the appellation of *The Gentleman*, I am proud to stile myself *A Blackguard*; a name, Sir, that would do you more credit both as a writer, and a man, than the title you have assumed. Humour, that genuine English production, is not the growth of a frippery age, nor founded on polished manners. It can only be cultivated by bold manly wits, such as Cervantes, Rabelais, Moliere, Swift, Gay, Arbuthnot, Fielding, Sterne, &c. &c. These, and such as these, are the Classicks of the School of Blackguard. In that school I have been bred, and have learnt to despise a delicacy of manners that produces effeminacy, and a nicety of taste that proves the weakness of the stomach. If these are models you disapprove, I here take my leave of you; but if English Virtue, English Sense, and English Humour, are meant to be recommended and encouraged by the Author of *The Gentleman*, he shall now and then, if he pleases, hear farther from one who is proud to own himself a friend to those qualities, and to subscribe himself

" A BLACKGUARD."

According to my Correspondent's definition, my idea of *a Gentleman*, and his idea of *a Blackguard*, constitute pretty nearly the same character. I think, indeed, he bears rather hard upon the FINE Gentleman of our age, and handles him with more roughness than so tender an animal provokes; yet it must be confessed that the writer's rusticity, becomes him, and (as Addison says of Virgil in his Georgicks) that "he tosses about his dung with an air of gracefulness." I cannot therefore dismiss his epistle without assuring him, that I wish for a continuance of his correspondence, as well as that of the Lady, who has favoured me with the following Letter.

To the GENTLEMAN.

SIR,

"DOES your total silence, concerning the female world, in your first number, proceed from contempt of the Sex? Do you think, with Mahomet, that Women are void of souls to be made happy in the next world; or, with a late Lord, that they are incapable of reason and common sense in the present? During the female reigns of Anne and Elizabeth, such doctrines would have

have been confidered as moral and political herefies, no lefs than religious: and they deferve, I think, as little encouragement in our times, when we fee a Queen Confort on the throne, at leaft equally amiable, and perhaps as wife in declining politicks, as the illuftrious regents above-mentioned were glorious in adminiftring them.

"Familiar Effays, Sir, have hitherto been peculiarly devoted to the fervice of the Ladies. Steele and Addifon ftept forth, like literary knights-errant, to refcue the fair from the dæmons of vice, and fpells of ignorance, endeavouring to render the toilet the altar of the Mufes, as well as the place of facrifice to the Graces. They thought the manners and principles of Women not unimportant to the happinefs of Men, and did not efteem it a difgrace to their parts or learning, to *write down* to the underftandings of female readers. Effays in general are, indeed, a kind of whipt-fillabub literature, not above the pitch of a mere houfewifely comprehenfion, and as becoming a part of the parlour-window furniture, as a tambour or a thread paper.

"I do not mean, Sir, by what I have faid, to accufe you of an elevation of ftyle and manner that throws us at a diftance, but rather to hint to you that a feeming a seeming neglect of the Ladies is not consistent with a writer, who stiles himself A Gentleman. Are you afraid that the distinguished propriety, elegance, and decent modesty of the females of the present age will afford you no room for animadversion? Or do you think them totally incorrigible? For my part, Sir, I believe them to be formed of the very same materials, as their mothers were before them, equally prone to err, and equally capable of amendment and instruction.

" Female virtues are certainly of consequence to the order of the moral world, and foibles ought not to be suffered to spring up neglected, and to over-run the mind like thorns and idle weeds: yet their delicacy is not to be wounded. Their follies must be tenderly probed, and the Essayist, like the Surgeon, should have the hand of a Lady. Shakespeare's Characters of Women, like the portraits of women by the President of our Royal Academy, are almost the only good ones drawn by men. There is a coarseness of outline, colour, and design, in most other artists, that make their Ladies appear not in the simple style of Cælia, Rosalind, Imogen, Desdemona, &c. but rather like men drest in women's cloaths. On these considerations therefore, while you, Sir, are engaged in painting the

Men,

Men, the Females shall, if you please, sit to Me; or if you will suppose yourself alone equal to finishing the main parts of the figure, you will at least allow that a Female hand is most likely to be correct in the drapery,

"You will, I doubt not, be extremely curious to be informed from whom this Letter proceeds, and vanity may perhaps incline you to suppose, that it is occasioned by some partiality to you or your writings. Your person, Sir, I do not know, nor at present desire to know, any more than I mean to discover my own. Whether I shall ever unveil myself, must appear hereafter. In the mean time, let your imagination draw as flattering a likeness of me, as Gentlemen-Quixotes picture to themselves of their several Dulcineas. Fancy me as young, handsome, rich, and agreeably accomplished, as your complexion, avarice, or vanity may require; and it is no matter how old, ugly, poor, and disagreeable I may really be, while I remain your assistant and humble servant,

"Incognita."

Till the Lady becomes acquainted with my name, character, and qualifications, she is desired to take it for granted that I am very tall, very well made,

made, exactly of the complection she likes best, and just in my prime. In the mean time I most thankfully accept her kind offer, and do not doubt but it will be agreeable to my fair readers. The ladies have indeed betrayed some partiality for male hair-dressers, stay-makers, mantua-makers, and even men-midwives: yet I think they will unbosom their failings more freely to one of their own sex; and any lady, labouring with spleen, malice, envy, ambition, avarice, or secret disorders of the mind, will be glad to be laid by a woman: especially as an able and experienced practitioner (meaning myself) will always attend, ready to assist in any very nice case or an accident.

THE GENTLEMAN.
NUMBER III.
Wednesday, July 26, 1775.

Obscurata diu populo bonus eruet, atque
Proferet in lucem speciosa vocabula rerum,
Quæ priscis memorata Catonibus atque Cethegis,
Nunc situs informis premit, et deserta vetustas.
Adsciscet nova, quæ genitor produxerit usus :
Vehemens, et liquidus, puroque simillimus amni,
Fundet opes, Latiumque beabit divite linguâ. HOR.

Mark where a bold expressive phrase appears,
Bright thro' the rubbish of a thousand years;
Command old words that long have slept, to wake,
Words, that wise Bacon, or brave Raleigh, spake;
Or bid the new be English, ages hence,
(For use will foster what's begot by sense;)
Pour the rich tide of Eloquence along,
Lucid and pure, yet vehement and strong,
With all the treasures of the Mother Tongue.*

LEARNING, like beaten gold, in proportion to its being more extended, becomes more superficial. Gross ignorance and profound erudition are now equally uncommon. Literature, no

---

* This imitation of the original Latin Motto is chiefly taken from the admirable Version of Pope; and the few alterations have not

no longer confined to colleges and cloifters, mixes itfelf in fome meafure with the commerce of the exchange, the exercifes of the camp, and the graces of the court: but the deep-read fcholar is a rarer character than ever. The main ftream of fcience, branching into numberlefs rivulets, grows fhallow, as well as clear. The ftores of learning are parcelled out by retail, and what was farcaftically faid of the reputed knowledge of our northern neighbours, is nearly applicable to that of the whole ifland. Every man has a mouthfull, but no man has a bellyfull.

This obfervation, on the ftate of learning in general, is almoft equally true in refpect to the leffer graces

---

not been made from a vain attempt at amendment, nor becaufe they bring the lines nearer to the fenfe of Horace, fo much as to accommodate the paffage to the matter of the Effay to which it is prefixed.

The lines in Pope run thus:

> Mark where a bold expreffive phrafe appears,
> Bright thro' the rubbifh of a thoufand years,
> Command old words, that long have flept, to wake,
> Words, that wife Bacon, or brave Raleigh, fpake;
> Or bid the new be Englifh, ages hence,
> (For ufe will father what's begot by fenfe;)
> Pour the full tide of Eloquence along,
> Serenely pure, and yet divinely ftrong,
> Rich with the treafures of each foreign tongue. POPE.

graces of Style and composition. That happy mediocrity, denied by Gods and Men to the writers of former ages, has been reserved for our own period. Few writers are barbarous and ungrammatical, or even unmusical, in their language; but very few are truly simple, nervous, or elegant. Some styles, like handsome faces, are spoilt by affectation, or ruined by varnish and extrinsick ornament; some are bloated with false pomp; some darkened by metaphysical abstract phraseology; and some enervated by dapper familiarities, and the cant jargon of drawing-rooms, horse-courses, and gaming-tables.

Purity of Style, like purity of manners, is not wholly practicable: languages, like men by whom they are framed, will be imperfect: yet every endeavour to trace the sources of corruption, tends to stop its progress. Living authors, as well as living manners, are at once the chief objects of our censure and imitation. The works of deceased writers, which we have been taught by tradition to applaud, are too seldom turned over; while the productions of our cotemporaries present themselves to our notice, oftener than their persons. He, who has talents to distinguish himself from

the

the crowd, has more followers than an ancient philofopher. A popular writer fets the fashion of Style, and the very herd of criticks, that wish to depreciate the value of his works, run after him. If an author arifes, whofe deep learning, and large imagination ftruggling for expreffion equal to his conceptions, tempt him to lengthen his periods, and fwell his phrafeology; if an intimate familiarity with the combinations of a dead language now and then betray him into too wide a deviation from the vernacular idiom; fuch a writer will have the mortification to fee the beauties of his Style diftorted by aukward imitation, and his errors (if in him they are errors) made ridiculous by aggravation. The language that, in his mafter hand, like a well-tuned inftrument, "difcourfes moft eloquent mufick," under their management utters nothing but difcord. The rattling of their periods and tumidity of their phrafes, like the noife of a drum or fwell of a bladder, are but fymptoms of their wind and emptinefs.

Ornament of diction, fays Quintilian, tho' the greateft of beauties, is only graceful, when it follows as it were of itfelf, not when it is purfued. Of all ornaments, a foreign ftructure of period, as it is the moft prejudicial to the genius of our language, appears the most studied and unnatural. An adopted word is but a partial and trifling innovation, and is often happily incorporated, when care is taken to naturalize the foreigner, by giving a national air to the turn of the phrase. Every language, more especially the English, has its idioms, which we should not register, with Grammarians and Lexicographers, among its irregularities, but with Poets and Orators, number among its beauties: To extirpate idiom from our tongue, would be like rooting up the old oaks, that are the glory and ornament of our country; or, to vary the allusion, to square the language of our ancient writers to the rigid rules of Roman or even French Syntax, would extinguish the genius of our Tongue, and give the whole a foreign air, like the labours of a tasteless improver, exchanging the luxuriance of nature, in our gardens, for clipt yews, strait walks, and formal parterres.

Perspicuity without meanness is pronounced by Aristotle to be the perfection of language, or, as he more nervously expresses it, the *virtue* of Style; to attain which, he recommends, as a principal instrument, the use of the most common words and phrases in a figurative signification; the familiarity of the terms rendering them clear, and the novelty

of

of their application giving them an air of elegance or dignity. The works of our old writers, profaick as well as poetical, abound with thefe homefpun metaphors, by which the loweft words increafe their confequence, or at leaft, like cyphers, raife the value of their neighbours. Sometimes, indeed, thefe popular tropes are carried to excefs, or ufed too licentioufly; yet they commonly breathe a magnificent fimplicity, and the whole conftruction is purely Englifh; a circumftance, like that which induced Cicero to recommend the ftudy of the ancient Roman authors to his pupils in oratory, urging, that whoever was well read in their productions, could not, were he even inclined to it, fpeak other than genuine Latin.

It will not, I hope, be imagined from what I have faid, that I think too lightly of the labours and genius of thofe learned philologifts, who, by compiling Grammars and Dictionaries, have endeavoured to give precifion and ftability to our Tongue. Their works, if properly confulted, are ufeful both to the learner and proficient; but if made the objects of their ftudy, rather than occafional affiftants, they will certainly be pernicious. The Grammars of living and dead languages are too often framed on different principles: in the latter

latter, all irregularities, for which an authority can be pleaded, are sanctified by a rule; while the other brands every idiom, or bold combination, as a licentious barbarism. No man ever learnt a language, living or dead, from a Grammar or Dictionary; but by reading the best authors, and partaking of the best conversation. He, who habituates himself to such studies and such society, without proposing to himself a particular model, will insensibly form a Style of his own; as in the mechanical part of writing, every man abandoning himself to his own fancy or powers, almost every man writes a different hand. A certain freedom of Style, a manly flow of language, will distinguish the authors of such a school; whose periods will not be divided into formal compartments, like the squares of a Mosaick pavement, exactly answering each other; but the members of a sentence, like the members of the human body, will seem to be put together with ease as well as symmetry, and equally framed for the purposes of elegance and strength.

As to Grammars and Dictionaries, though not administering to the foundation of our tongue, they may certainly be of great use to contribute to its preservation. They are a kind of scaffold erected

by

by skilful workmen, after our language has been completely built, to repair the ruins of time, and to keep the venerable structure from further decay. The last great English Dictionary will remain, as long as the English Tongue shall remain, a monument of the learning and genius of its author; and I cannot better enforce the utility of the studies recommended in this paper, than by concluding it with an extract from the admirable Preface to that work; a Preface, which at once delivers the precepts, and affords the example, of a pure and eloquent Style.

——" I have studiously endeavoured to collect examples and authorities from the writers before the Restoration, whose works I regard as *the wells of English undefiled*, as the pure sources of genuine diction. Our language, for almost a century, has, by the concurrence of many causes, been gradually departing from its original *Teutonick* character, and deviating towards a Gallick structure and phraseology, from which it ought to be our endeavour to recall it, *by making our ancient volumes the groundwork of Style*, admitting among the additions of later times, only such as may supply real deficiencies, such as are readily adopted by the

genius

geuius of our tongue, and incorporate eafily with our native idioms.

————" From the authors which rofe in the time of Elizabeth, a fpeech might be formed adequate to all the purpofes of ufe and elegance. If the language of theology were extracted from Hooker and the tranflation of the Bible; the terms of natural knowledge from Bacon; the phrafes of policy, war, and navigation from Raleigh; the dialect of poetry and fiction from Spenfer and Sidney; and the diction of common life from Shakefpeare, few ideas would be loft to mankind, for want of Englifh words in which they might be expreffed."

The GENTLEMAN.

NUMBER IV.

Monday, August 7, 1775.

Age vero, ne semper forum, subsellia, rostra, curiamque meditere, quid esse potest in otio aut jucundius, aut magis proprium humanitatis, quàm sermo facetus, ac nullâ in re dutis? Hoc enim uno præstamus vel maxime feris, quòd colliquimur inter nos, & quòd exprimere dicendo sensa possumus.
CICERO.

Well then, not to dwell on the Bar, the Bench, the Pulpit, or the Parliament, what can, in our hours of relaxation, be more agreeable, or better suited to our nature, than chearful, and elegant Conversation? For in this consists our chief pre-eminence over the brute creation, that we can converse with each other, and communicate our sentiments by Speech.

To the Author of The GENTLEMAN.

*E*CCE ITERUM! the Blackguard again! your last paper has roused me, and while you are learnedly commenting on the Style of Writing, give me leave, Sir, to throw in a word or two on a
matter

matter of more immediate consequence to the comfort and happiness of life—the Style of Conversation. I don't mean the rounding of sentences, or saying pretty things prettily, or fine things finely, or backing your horses, like Mrs. Flourigig, in the midst of a speech, for the sake of turning the corner of a period; but the downright communication of our thoughts to each other, the life and soul of all social intercourse, the first purpose of meeting and company, and the great distinction between our species and the rest of the animal creation.

"Speak, that I may know thee." said the wise man of old; but according to the prescribed use of speech in polite company, it is impossible for us to come at the least knowledge of each other; not on account of our using speech for the purpose of dissimulation, but because it is ungenteel forsooth, to discover, in company, that you have any knowledge at all; or for any one person to speak above five seconds at a time, or above five words in a breath.

Tediousness and Prosing in Conversation, is an abominable practice, I allow; but no man ever dealt half so disagreeably in that figure of rhetorick, which, I think, Swift calls the *Circumbendibus*,

as

as the fops and flirts of the present age now deal in the abrupt, snip-snap manner of abandoning a subject before three syllables have been said upon it; flying from one question to another, as if each had been started for the sake of quitting it immediately, or as if the very ghost of good sense was to be laid in all good company. Conversation was intended as a kind of traffick of mental commodities, but nobody now dare open their budget: and lest nature should set some tongues a going, the puppies of the world have, from time to time, contrived to put a kind of gag in our mouths, by inventing certain terms calculated to turn every man to ridicule, who will venture to deliver his sentiments, or disclose his mind for the information or entertainment of the company. If you attempt to tell a story, one puppy puts his hand to his cheek, and cries *Patch!* implying, it seems, that the tale is old, and smells of *Joe Miller*; and if you continue your narration a minute and half, another puppy turns to a monkey next him, and whispers " what a *bore!* or *boar!*" for I don't know how they spell their nonsense; but (take it which way you will) it is intended to convey an idea of tediousness, and to compare the speaker to a hog or a gimlet : but sure, Sir, such wretches are

themselves

themselves the greatest enemies to good company; mere dampers to the mind, wet blankets to the imagination, and extinguishers of good sense and good humour. Taciturnity is the great vice of Englishmen, and it would be more expedient to devise methods to prevail on them to throw off that reserve that freezes their conversation, than to study these poor meagre inventions to shut up every man's light, like a dark lanthorn, within his own bosom. A bold free spirit, it is true, will leap these fences; but it is hard, methinks, that a plain modest man should be stopt in the high road of conversation, and not suffered to go on without interruption.

I love humour and pleasantry, Sir, as well as the merriest man in the kingdom; but give me leave to inform these fine gentlemen, that it is a melancholy symptom, when they cannot bear the serious pursuit of any subject for two minutes together. Humour itself, if good for any thing, is serious at the bottom; but what provokes me, is, that these cuckows are as grave as stoicks, and hold it a kind of treason to laugh; for the old folly is revived, which almost began to grow obsolete in our ancient comedies, of being *gentleman-like and melancholy.* Conversation being a kind of short extempore compofition, all fevere cenfure of what falls from us, prophanenefs and indecency excepted, is ridiculous: not only fenfe, but for the fake of fenfe, even nonfenfe, fhould be tolerated; for a man who is always afraid of uttering what may be interpreted to be nonfenfe, will not give his underftanding fair play; and he will often let the immediate occafion, that would have given grace and force to his obfervations, pafs by. He will feem, like an aukward militia-man, difcharging his folitary blunderbufs, long after the reft of the corps; or at beft, fuppofing his words to have real weight and fterling value, they will come upon us untowardly, like diftant thunder, which does not reach our ears, till long after the flafh has taught us to expect it.

By attending and obferving Modern Converfation, one would be tempted to imagine that it was one of the firft principles of politenefs, to drive all fentiment and fcience out of fociety. Every thing relative to a man's peculiar concerns, in which he might fuppofe his friends and acquaintance to take fome little intereft, is deemed impertinent; and every thing relative to knowledge is deemed pedantick. Formerly the honeft bottle forced fome rational and fpirited fallies, even from the moſt riotous company; but the milkſops of our age keep themſelves ſober, till the cards or dice relieve them from the cruel neceſſity of endeavouring to amuſe each other by Converſation. In the mean time, to put a curb on the fancy, leſt the little genius they have ſhould grow reſtive, and run away with them, they deviſe theſe miſerable mechanical pieces of ridicule, as reſtraints on the freedom of ſociety. I am rather an old fellow, perhaps ſomewhat peeviſh, and I confeſs it often puts me quite out of patience; when a man cries *Patch!* at one of my ſtories, I am almoſt provoked to give him a ſlap on the face; and when a puppy ſeems to meaſure my words with a ſtop watch, and at the end of a few ſeconds cries, *Bore!* I am almoſt ready to call him out for his rudeneſs and impertinence.

We have loſt the noble art of antiquity of writing elegant compoſitions in the form of Dialogue. No wonder: for what dialogue can appear natural, when ſuppoſed to proceed from the mouths of men who will diſcourſe on no ſubject, who preclude all pleaſantries, as vulgar, and ſuperſede all knowledge as pedantick? As to ſentiment, it might find as much quarter in a modern comedy from a modern critick, as from our puny
eſtabliſhers

establishers of the laws of Converfation. The heart and the head are equally unconcerned, and to seem to know any thing, or to feel any thing, are alike breaches of politenefs. But furely, Sir, all this is directly oppofite to the warmth and plainnefs of our old national character: we were wont, like Shakefpeare's Claudio, to fpeak home and to the purpofe. If a man's mind is full of ideas, why not let them run over, and water the barren underftandings, or refresh the fruitful wits, of the company? And indeed, a man himfelf fcarce knows what ftuff he has in his thoughts, till he has drawn them out into difcourfe, and often forms his own opinion according to the impreffions that his words feem to make on his hearers. Anfwers too are produced, frequently given with more fhrewdnefs on the fpot, than on further confideration; and truth, as well as wit, is ftruck out by collifion. I don't mean to confider every company as a tinder-box, and to fet argument and repartee, like flint and fteel, perpetually ftriking againft each other; yet if a fpark is now and then lighted up, why fhould the officious hand of dulnefs be authorized, by fuppofed politenefs, to extinguifh it? Converfation is mentioned by Lord Bacon, (as wife a man, Sir, as the wifeft of our *macaronies*,) among

among the chief benefits of friendſhip, "making day-light in the underſtanding, out of darkneſs and confuſion of thoughts;" and as you adorned your laſt paper by an extract from a learned Modern, give me leave to wind up the bottom of my looſe thoughts on *Converſation,* with a paſſage tranſcribed from that great Chancellor and Philoſopher.

" Whoever hath his mind fraught with many thoughts, his wit and underſtanding do clarifie and break up in the communicating and diſcourſing with another; he toſſeth his thoughts more eaſily, he marſhalleth them more orderly, he ſeeth how they look when they are turned into words: finally, he waxeth wiſer than himſelf, and that more by an hour's diſcourſe, than by a day's meditation. It was well ſaid by Themiſtocles to the King of Perſia, *That ſpeech was like cloth of Arras, opened and put abroad; whereby the imagery doth appear in figure, whereas in thought they lie but as in packs.* Neither is the fruit of friendſhip, of opening the underſtanding, reſtrained only to ſuch friends as are able to give a man counſel; (they indeed are beſt) but even without that a man learneth of himſelf, and bringeth his own thoughts to light, and whetteth his wits as againſt a ſtone, which itſelf cuts not. In a word, a man were better relate

himſelf

himself to a statue or picture, than to suffer his thoughts to pass in smother."

" Conference, says Lord Coke also, is the life of study: Conference, says Lord Bacon again, makes a ready man, and if he confer little, he had need have a present wit."—In short, Sir, Conversation is the great source of pleasure and information in society, and whoever contributes to dam it up, should be strenuously opposed by the rest of mankind. But to suffer a bye word, a low cant term, to deprive us of the means of entertainment and intelligence, is the meanest pusillanimity, and sacrificing good sense at the shrine of folly and nonsense.

I must beg leave, therefore, by an *index expurgatorius*, to banish *Patch* and *Bore* from the modern vocabulary; not merely on account of the barbarity of the terms, but for the evil tendency of the ridiculous something, or less than nothing, implied by them; for they are not only framed by blockheads destitute of meaning in themselves, but calculated to kill the seeds of good sense and humanity in other people. I am,

    S I R,
     Your's as before,
       A BLACKGUARD.

THE GENTLEMAN.

NUMBER V.

Wednesday, October 25, 1775.

Proximus huic, longo sed proximus intervallo. VIRG.

The *next* 'tis true; and yet 'tis clear,
Altho' the *next*, it is not *near*.

THOUGH I did not on the commencement of this undertaking engage to appear before the Publick at any certain stated periods, yet it might not unreasonably be presumed by the occasional reader, that I should at least adhere in some degree to the usual practice of an Occasional Writer. In the small circle of those, who did me the honour to peruse the foregoing numbers, my long silence has, I find, given rise to various conjectures. Some have

have not fcrupled to pronounce me really & *bonâ fide* deceafed; while others have contented themfelves with lamenting my metaphorical departure from the literary world, faying, that my fmall kilderkin of wit was entirely exhaufted. Others, again have afferted, that during the fummer months, I was, like my betters, retired into the country. Many concurring in this opinion, have however attributed my filence to fome accident attending my retirement or peregrinations. Some have reprefented me on horfeback, like the Taylor riding to Brentford, and have cruelly diflocated my collarbone by a fall; fome have fhot me with a fpringgun, or ftuck me in a man-trap, like Gulliver in a. marrowbone; fome have caft me away on an inland-navigation; and fome have buried me alive in a cavern of the Peak.

I have now the pleafure to inform my friends that I am alive, and hope they will find me alive and merry. The truth is, I have been in the country; and though I cannot, like the inimitable Spectator, indulge myfelf in a feries of rural lucubrations; though I cannot extract entertainment from the hiftory of an henrooft, or pen an agreeable differtation upon haycocks; yet before I meet the Parliament in London, and fet up my reft in town for the winter, I will give a short account of my first visit during the summer recess. This publication however is not without the privity and good liking of mine host. Let me not be blamed therefore for a breach of the laws of hospitality!

My old schoolfellow and college acquaintance, Sir Jocelyn Hearty, having long importuned me to pass two or three weeks with him in the country, about the beginning of August I set out for his seat, and towards the conclusion of the second day, found myself nearly at the end of my journey. Within two or three miles of the mansion-house, I encountered several horse-men whose seat appeared uncommonly loose and unsteady; some in small parties, hanging over their horses, and seeming in earnest conversation with each other; some galloping furiously after, dropping whips, and hats, and wigs, by the way, and shouting as they past, to denote their good fellowship, and hail their acquaintance. Upon turning into the grounds, which lead directly to the house, my ears were saluted with a loud vocal chorus, which however quickly subsided, but was almost as quickly renewed, and thus rose and fell by turns, till I was arrived at the gate. Entering the hall, I found it strewed with honest rusticks, fast asleep, in their

boots

boots and great coats. A saloon on each side of the hall was filled with benches and long tables, at which a jovial company still kept their places, drinking, toasting, and singing.

My friend, it seems, was already retired. An old servant, however, took me under his protection, and provided me with every necessary accommodation till the next morning. About noon I was introduced to Sir Jocelyn, whom I found in his dressing-room, with a bowl before him, containing a composition of milk, nutmeg, and brandy, which he called *a Doctor*. This Doctor is, it seems, always called in on the morrow of these joyous festivities, and though not regular, may boast as numerous a set of patients, and a practice as extensive, as any of the Faculty. After a hearty shake by the hand, and a few other civilities, the Baronet informed me, that he and his friends of yesterday had been getting drunk *according to act of parliament*. Having formerly been a student of the law, I expressed some surprise at not being able to recollect so particular a chapter in the statute book. "It is one of the best of them all, for all "that, said Sir Jocelyn: and yet it is but a new "law neither, and I had the honour to assist at the "passing it. The *Grenville* Bill, my friend! "Since,

"Since that Bill paſt into a law, we dare not give
"a gill of wine, or a tiff of punch, before the
"election; but it is fit we ſhould entertain our
"friends handſomely ſome time after it is over,
"that the freeholders may ſee we do not forget
"them, and remember us hereafter accordingly."
I could not help ſmiling at ſo ingenious an expoſition of the ſtatute, telling my friend that the ſoundneſs of his law put me in mind of Foigard's logick, "if you receive it before-hand it is a bribe;
"but if you take it afterwards, is is only a gratification."

A few days after, Sir Jocelyn told me, if it was a matter of indifference to me which way I might ride that morning, he ſhould be very glad of my company to a village at about eight miles diſtance. "But I muſt quit you at the town's end, ſays he,
"for I am engaged to dinner, and on particular
"buſineſs. We have a Meeting of the Juſtices." The chief buſineſs of this meeting, it ſeems, was to ſign Licences for the Publick Houſes for the year enſuing. This buſineſs was fortunately diſpatched before dinner; fortunately, I ſay, becauſe their Worſhips ſhewed themſelves ſo ſincerely well inclined to promote the intereſt of thoſe, whoſe callings they met to authoriſe, that it
would

would not have been prudent to poftpone an operation for which their very zeal might difqualify them. In fhort, after a joyous day, Sir Jocelyn rode home rather quicker than he went, and we faw no more of him till the next morning.

In about a week more however he was again called forth to a Turnpike Meeting. Sir Jocelyn, ever ready to accommodate his friends, and ferve the Publick, duly attended; but the road under confideration proved fo execrable, and fo many difficulties occurred concerning the propofals for repairing it, that the Committee fat till midnight, and did not rife till they had debated the matter, like the antient Germans, both drunk and fober.

The Races and the Affizes, being each a kind of affembly of the whole county, it was impoffible for the Baronet and his family to be abfent from either. On two different days of the Races were entered two horfes belonging to Sir Jocelyn. Both ftarted, but their fortune was as various as their colours. The firft day, his bald-faced grey horfe, North, won the odds againft the field, carried off the King's Plate, and was victorious; but on the fecond day his brown horfe, Orator, took ruft, ran out of the courfe, and was diftanced. Sir Jocelyn and his friends, after the example of the Ancients, celebrated

one

one of these events, and lamented the other, exactly in the same manner. The flowing bowls were crowned again and again in honour of the winner, and the cup of affliction ran over in sorrow for the loser.

At the Assizes, Sir Jocelyn was Foreman of the Grand Jury. So many bills were presented, that the several members of the Inquest, exhausted by their uncommon fatigue, required a more than ordinary recruit. It is no wonder therefore that, having duly dispatched in sober sadness the business of the nation, the honest country gentlemen relaxed their gravity, and converting their solemn assembly to a merry meeting, protracted their sitting after supper till daylight.

An old boon companion of my acquaintance used to say, that getting tipsy was one of the pleasantest things in the world, but that nothing was so irksome and painful than its necessary consequence, getting sober again. This was exactly the case with Sir Jocelyn. The text of every evening was mirth and jollity, but the comment of the morrow-morning was sorrow and sickness. The hunting season commenced some little time before I departed. Every hare or fox that had been killed in the morning, was revived at night, and again

run

run down in full cry. The exercise of the chase was less laborious than the festivity of the evening. Politicks took their turn also. America was floated with lakes of claret, and the blockade of Boston caused many an head-ach. On one of these occasions, seeing my worthy friend in much pain, I could not refrain from a short and affectionate expostulation, regretting that an excellent understanding should be drowned in liquor, and the best of men rendered a martyr to his own hospitality and benevolence. " Ah, my dear friend,
" said Sir Jocelyn, with his hand pressed upon his
" temples, you Town Gentlemen imagine that we
" lead very quiet, idle, lives in the Country : but
" take my word for it, that it requires a very good
" estate, and a very good constitution, to support,
" as one ought to do, the character of a Country
" Gentleman."

THE GENTLEMAN.

NUMBER VI.

Monday, December 4, 1775.

*Respicere exemplar vitæ morumque jubebo
Doctum imitatorem, et veras hinc ducere voces.* HOR.

On Nature's pattern too I'll bid him look,
And copy Manners from her living book.

Colman's Art of Poetry.

To the GENTLEMAN.

SIR,

SINCE you have announced your arrival in town, I hope you intend to demonstrate by some future papers, that you are a frequenter of the Theatre. I love the Playhouse, and am one of those plain folks that dine early enough to attend the rising of the curtain. I do not sit down to table at six, prolong the last course till eight or nine, and then perhaps crack my head with cracking a bottle, or rattling a dice-box, till eight or nine the next morning. I hope therefore, since with the
bulk

bulk of my countrymen, I take an intereſt in theſe entertainments, that you will, like your predeceſſor-eſſayiſts, gratify us with ſome ſound criticiſms on the Drama: found criticiſms, I ſay; no flimſy panegyrick, or groſs abuſe, praiſing or reviling one writer or performer for the purpoſe of raiſing or debaſing another; but tracing and enforcing the real principles of the Drama; and if examples, for the ſake of illuſtration, muſt now and then be given, give them from the Claſſick Dead! for praiſe or cenſure of the Living is commonly nauſeous, commonly ſuſpicious. The Dead too (no offence to the preſent generation!) are our more intimate acquaintance.

I do not mean however to depreciate the talents of the Living. No Sir, you will find that the main ſcope of this letter is to encourage cotemporary merit, and to repreſs the petulance, and expoſe the futility, of common-place criticiſm. Writers, who endeavour to effect their purpoſe by methods merely mechanical, are juſtly denied the Palm of Genius. Ought Criticks then to comment by line and rule, and to decide by a receipt? If Criticiſm be the handmaid of the Muſe, ſhe might ſurely catch ſomething of her air and ſpirit, rather than rip up the caſt cloaths of her miſtreſs, at once to

ſteal

steal the pattern, and find fault with the fashion. In a word, her labours should be directed to promote the arts, rather than to dishearten the professors; and though it must naturally fall out that more can see and read than those who write, and paint, &c. yet since they who hazard their observations in publick, in some measure become artists themselves, they should take care to found those observations on the basis of candour, taste, and good sense. At present the press swarms with Criticks. A louse, say the naturalists, is a very lousy animal; and there is not a lousy author in town, especially a Dramatick Author, that has not fifty lousy Criticks on his back. These bloodsuckers have no doubt their use, and may serve to correct the too sanguine imagination of an author: But I beg leave to mention a few instances, wherein I think they contribute to weaken and to impoverish genius.

The first canon of Modern Criticism (and indeed it has been a favourite topick ever since the Flood) is the degeneracy of the present age. This is the grand æra of Dulness: Genius, they cry, is extinct. Shakespeare, Jonson, and Fletcher; Wycherly, Congreve, and Vanbrugh, are no more! —True; and the present writers, such as they are, will

will hereafter at leaſt have that claim to applauſe. They will be no more.—But a good Play, ſay the Criticks, is ſo ſcarce, ſo very ſcarce a commodity! —Granted. When was it otherwiſe? Allowing for a moment, that every old piece in Dodſley's Collection is excellent, how few are ſuch pieces to thoſe which were then written and exhibited, whoſe wit and ſpirit has not been ſufficient to keep them ſweet, and alive, for the delight and entertainment of the preſent generation! From the days of Æſchylus to yeſterday, few writers have been equal to the hard taſk of a good Tragedy; to write a Comedy is a ſerious matter; and even an excellent Farce-monger (ſays Diderot) is no ordinary character. I have looked upon the Stage for a long, long ſeries of time, and without flattery to the preſent race of Dramatiſts, I will venture to pronounce that the laſt five and twenty years, or thereabouts, have produced more plays likely to deſcend to poſterity, than the five and twenty immediately preceding. I do not mean to pay my court to any particular author; I have thrown the compliment among them, and let each of them take as much of it as he may think falls to his ſhare.

To point out antique merit to the Moderns, as an object of emulation, is wiſe and laudable; but

to

to set it up, like the gallows, to terrify and gibbet poor culprits, that venture on the high road of letters, is impolitick and ungenerous. Comparisons are commonly invidious, yet there are a kind of comparisons still more odious than those between the Antients and Moderns—I mean those drawn between Moderns and Moderns. Wits, as well as Beauties, are naturally fond of pulling caps, and mangling the reputations of each other. But shall the sober Critick, who ought to keep down their vanity, and quell their arrogance, shall *He*, as it were *ex cathedrâ*, give a sanction to their squabbles, or throw additional weight into that scale, which success and self-conceit have perhaps already made too heavy? Let every successful writer triumph in his turn, yet do not chain his fellow-authors to the wheels of his chariot; but rather let it be the office of a Critick, like the slave of the Antients, to bid him remember that he is mortal.

But the most offensive weapon of Modern Criticism is some *reigning word*, with which every literary Rifleman arms himself, and does dreadful execution. The two leading monosyllables of the House of Commons are not more powerful than such *a word*, be it what it may, while it remains
formidable

formidable by being in fashion. I am old enough to remember when the word Low was this Scare-crow. *Genteel* Comedy, and the *politest* Literature, were in univerfal requeft; and every writer who attempted to be *comick*, dreaded the imputation of buffoonery. If a piece had ftrong humour—Oh, Sir, it's damned *low!*—was its fentence of condemnation. At length, however, the word Low has been reftored to favour, and the term SENTIMENT in its turn has fallen into difgrace. "To anatomife a character, and fee what breeds about the heart," had formerly its merit; but now this diffection of the human mind has loft its advocates and admirers: *Sentimental stuff* is the phrafe; and he who dares to approve a fcene, where the courfe of the ftory apparently leads the author to exhibit Paffion rather than Humour, is condemned for an old-fafhioned dunce and a coxcomb. Grofs drolleries, or dull moralities, (*moralities* let me call them!) are equally reprehenfible: but Humour is not to be cenfured merely becaufe it is *low*, nor *fentiment* to be banifhed when it feems to exhibit the workings of the heart. With the Ancient Criticks, the *Manners* and *Sentiments*, held an equal rank in the Drama:

Drama: each alike excellent, while they were each alike *characteriſtick*.

After ſuch a free cenſure of the modern coinage of cant terms in the Critical Vocabulary, if I might be allowed to give currency to a word, I would endeavour to renew one, that is as old as the creation—NATURE!—the ſterling bullion of NATURE!—Let the Criticks ceaſe to enquire whether the Humour be *low*, or the piece *ſentimental*; let them examine whether it be *natural!* But let the admirer and imitator of Nature alſo be on his guard, not to fall into inſipidity, or to indulge the minute touches of a Dutch pencil. Let your outline be bold, tho' ſimple; and fill it as richly, and colour it as highly, as you pleaſe; always taking care to avoid *extravaganza*, and " to hold, as it were, the Mirror up to *Nature!*" This is no curb upon the imagination. Caliban is as natural as Hamlet.

Compoſition and Criticiſm are ſo nearly allied, that in making ſtrictures upon one I have been betrayed almoſt unawares into ſpeaking of the other. Narrowneſs in each, *manneriſts* in writing and *manneriſts* in criticiſm, are equally my averſion. The wretched fellow, that could paint nothing but a roſe, was not in my opinion more contemptible, than

than the cuckow who can repeat nothing but *low* or *sentimental*. The wide field of *Nature* gives scope for that *variety*, which ever diftinguifhes an æra of genius. Never was there a period, wherein excellent authors flourifhed, but their feveral manners were as different as their faces; nay, a good author poffeffes a verfatility of talent, not only keeping him above the fervile imitation of others, but enabling him in great meafure to vary from himfelf. Yet there is another vice of Criticks, which I forgot to mention before. I mean their perpetually recurring to every writer's firft production, and fettling it as the ftandard of his genius, as if they dreaded his cultivating more than one fpot of Parnaffus. To compare a man with himfelf, difadvantageoufly too, is of all comparifons the moft mortifying: but mortification is no more the main bufinefs of the Critick, than torture fhould be the ftudy of the Surgeon, tho' fome pain will of neceffity follow both their operations.

To conclude, Sir, while I recommend the Drama to your notice, I mean to warn you from falling into the vulgar errors of ordinary commentators. And I hope you will take warning. But if you go on, gingling the bells of Panegyrick, or wading through the mire of Abufe, in the beaten track of

Modern Criticifm, I wifh that your remarks may perifh, as fpeedily as the lie of the day, with which they appear; and that your Effays may be configned to oblivion, with the News-papers in which they are printed.

In hopes of better things from your candour and difcernment, I remain your old friend, and old correfpondent,

THE BLACKGUARD.

TERRÆ-FILIUS.

PUBLISHED DAILY

During the Encænia at OXFORD,

In HONOUR of the PEACE.

MDCCLXIII.

☞ *The following Letter, though written by another
hand, and without the privity of* TERRÆ-
FILIUS, *is yet prefixt to his papers now repub-
lished, as an Introduction, or short Preface,
conveying a just idea of the Design of the Author,
and the Nature of the Undertaking.*

To the PRINTER *of the* ST. JAMES'S CHRONICLE.

SIR,

AS the TERRÆ-FILIUS is to be reviv'd at the
ENCÆNIA now held at Oxford, the following explanation of that character may be agreeable
to some of your readers.

TERRÆ-FILIUS is a student who writes a satyr
upon the members of the University during the
Festival, and taxes them with any *faux pas*, or irregularities, they may have committed; a sort of a
licensed Pasquin for the time. He takes his title
from the old Roman phrase TERRÆ-FILIUS, which
among them signified an obscure or unknown person; it neither being proper nor adviseable that the
author of the censures usually thrown out under
this character should be publickly known. It is
confidently reported, the celebrated Mr. C——ll
is gone down to assist therein.

P 4 As

As the word ENCÆNIA alfo may probably puzzle the unlettered part of your readers, it will not be amifs to inform them, that it fignifies an ANNIVERSARY FEAST, held by the Primitive Chriftians in commemoration of the day on which their Churches were founded, and fince ufed to denote any Annual Feftival. The money out of which the expences of the prefent ENCÆNIA at Oxford are to be defrayed, was originally left, if I miftake not, to New College, by their generous benefactor Lord Crew, and was formerly laid out in what is called a GAUDY, from the Latin word *Gaudeo*, to rejoice, that is to fay, *fpent in eating and drinking*. But for thefe thirteen years paft, the College, with a difintereftednefs which does them the higheft Honour, have beftowed the Legacy on the Univerfity, to be by them laid out in defraying the expences of an Annual Mufical Entertainment, or fuch other *Celebrity* as fhall be likely to render the Univerfity famous, and increafe the number of its Patrons, by drawing a concourfe of Gentry and Nobility there, who are always complimented on thefe occafions with Academical Honours fuitable to their Rank. The Feftivities of this year derive additional luftre from the Inftallation of their Chancellor, the Right Hon. the Earl of Litchfield.

Temple,   Z. T.
July 4, 1763.

TERRÆ-FILIUS.

NUMBER I.

Tuesday, July 5, 1763.

Audire, atque Togam jubeo componere, *quisquis*
Ambitione malâ, aut argenti pallet amore ;
Quisquis luxuriâ, tristive superstitione,
Aut alio mentis morbo calet : huc, propius me,
Dum doceo insanire omnes, ves ordine adite! Hor.

Hear all, I charge you, of this learned Town,
Hear, and with rev'rence fold your Classick Gown!
Whether a Priest of luscious d'sposition,
Or, Layman overrun by Superstition,
What'er disease inflames your minds, draw near,
With rev'rence fold your Classick Gowns, and hear!
Ambitious avaricious, gay, or sad,
All to a man, my text is, all stark mad!

TO all whom it may concern, I the great TERRÆ-FILIUS, the redoubted Academical Satyrist, the terror of old and young, male and female, graduates and undergraduates, gownsmen and townsmen, matriculated and unmatriculated, send greeting. I am come, Ladies and
Gentlemen,

Gentlemen, according to ancient custom, to be one of the principal Actors in the Celebrities of the present Term. You have heard, without doubt, of the noble exploits of my predecessors, those bold assertors of the Freedom of Speech, and the Liberty of the Press. Though the degeneracy of the times, and the numberless innovations in the ancient customs and usages of the University will not permit me, after the manner of my ancestors, to enter the Theatre, and pour forth the torrent of my Family Eloquence from the Rostrum, yet I am resolved, not to be put to silence. *My wisdom shall cry aloud in the streets, though no man regardeth it.* I will erect my temporary Stage, like the itinerant practitioners in physick, in the highway; I will *make a speech without doors.* If I am forbid to mount the regular Pulpit, I do not doubt of having as numerous followers as other Field-Preachers. I am determined, at all events, to maintain the Honour, and assert the Privileges of my family; and make no doubt of being able to prove myself a Chip of the Old Block.

The method I have taken of announcing my intentions, by Advertisements in the London Papers, and Oxford Journal has, I find, created the utmost consternation among all ranks and
degrees

degrees of people in this famous Town and University. The Mayor and Corporation, I am informed were firſt ſeiſed with the pannick fit, and held a council extraordinary on this occaſion; when it was taken into conſideration, whether they ſhould put me into the Stocks, ſend me to the Houſe of Correction, or bind me over to appear at the next Quarter Seſſions. At length however it was held to be an Univerſity-Buſineſs, and to fall more properly under the cogniſance of the Houſe of Convocation. From the Body Corporate therefore my cauſe was removed, by a new kind of *Certiorari*, to the Body Academical. The Right Honourable the Chancellor, I am told, is alarmed, and thinks of iſſuing a formal prohibition. The Learned and Reverend the Vice-Chancellor, I hear, has declared that he will not grant his *Imprimatur* to my Works: and the wiſe heads in Golgotha have laid their Sculls together about me and my paper. That formidable lawyer, and learned gentleman, the VENERIAN Profeſſor, it is confidently aſſerted, is conſulting the Archives, to prepare a SOLEMN LECTURE on the two tremendous Statutes *De Contumeliis Compeſcendis*, and *De Famoſis Libellis*. The Publick Orator, they ſay, is drawing up an Harangue in the ſtyle and ſpirit of *Quouſque tandem?*

tandem? and the Poetry Profeffor is writing a Poem againſt me. It is further added, that the name of TERRÆ-FILIUS himſelf, as ſoon as it is certainly known, will be regiſtered in the BLACK BOOK; and he himſelf, like moſt of his fore-fathers, will be publickly expelled:—That his poor printer will be trained after a Beadle, as big as Pope Beaver, into the Vice-Chancellor's Court, and in ſpite of the Statute *De Privilegiis Urbis et Univerſitatis ſimul non fruendis*, have the honour of an Academical *Mittimus* to the Caſtle or *Bocardo*.

Some few, however, who fancy that they ſee deeper than the ſurface, and that they have more penetration than their neighbours, affect to know me and my intentions better. The dreadful ſound of the name I have aſſumed, which has alarmed the vulgar, as that of *Raw-head-and-bloody-bones* ſerves as a bug-bear for children, theſe confident gentlemen affect to conſider as a mere ſcare-crow ſet up to fright the few ſhallow daws and chattering pies of the Univerſity, while my words, however big and ſonorous, are as innocent as the noiſe of a cherry-clapper. They affect to laugh at thoſe who have conceived horrible ideas of me, and cry out, when they hear that TERRÆ-FILIUS is coming, that *there is a lion in the way*. TERRÆ-FILIUS, they

they pretend, is not that tremendous animal he was wont to be. Lion as he is, he has filed his teeth, and pared his claws, and though he may venture to lift up his voice, and make *the wide forest tremble at his roar*, yet like Shakefpear's Lion, he will roar as gently as any nightingale.

Be this as it may, whether I fhall prove myfelf a Literary Hornet, a downright Academical Wafp, or merely an innocent *Humble-bee*, with a fmall fting by way of defence, or *melius non tangere*, in my tail; whether my ftyle will be more agreeable to the genius of our modern ENCÆNIA, or the old *Saturnalia*; whether I fhall pour forth from my fmall cruet of wit and humour the oil of Panegyrick, or the vinegar of Invective and Satire; in whatever manner I may write or fpeak; ftill, Gentlemen, I muft infift on it, that I have a natural, an uncontrovertible right to appear at thefe Solemnities, a right eftablifhed by the ancient forms of the Univerfity, and recognifed by the Statutes. The celebrities appendant and appurtenant to the *Act-Term*, every man muft acknowledge, would be imperfect without the admiffion of fuch a character as that I have undertaken to fuftain; a character as neceffary to enliven the gravity of folemn convocations, formal proceffions, long harangues, dull
                                                                            difputations,

disputations, and oratorios *most musical, most melancholy*, as the introduction of the Fool among the personages of the Old Comedy, or that merry gentleman Master Punch among the wooden Kings and Queens' at a Puppet-Shew. It is the peculiar nature also of seasons of festivity, to strike out sallies of Wit, and indulge strokes of Satire, which give no more annoyance to the general merriment, than illuminations and fireworks on a night of rejoicing, though perhaps some queer old gentleman may be alarmed at the crackers bouncing about his ears, the serpents hissing at his tail, or a squib whizzing in his periwig.

In an age less productive of innovations than the present, I should indeed be surprized that when the Celebration of the Peace has occasioned a kind of *Publick Act*, no person, properly qualified should be called upon by the Heads of the University to officiate in the capacity of TERRÆ-FILIUS in the Theatre; or at least if so essential a Personage as TERRÆ-FILIUS should be by our Academical Licensers and Chamberlains silenced and forbid to appear on the scene, I am still more surprized that the character of *Publick Orator* also should not be wiped out of the *Dramatis Personæ*. His rattling Eloquence and my Sprightlinefs, (or, if you please

to

to call it fo, *Impertinence*) fhould accompany one another as naturally as thunder and lightning. To have all praife and no fatire, all fweet and no four, is to make your punch without lemon. The province of Publick Orator, we know by experience, is wholly Panegyrick; that is (the cafe of the prefent company always excepted) to fay every thing of a man but the truth; whereas the very nature and fpirit of my office demands, that although the truth fhould not be told at all times, yet at this particular feafon, I may tell the truth, the whole truth, and fometimes perhaps, a little more than the truth; and though truth in general is well known to be at the bottom of the well, yet on thefe occafions, it may be pumped up, be the fprings ever fo foul and muddy, till it runs clear, and dealt out among you by pails and buckets full.

The Reverend Dr. BROWN, a worthy member and llluftrious ornament of a Sifter Univerfity, in a differtation lately publifhed, wherein he has drawn all the rudiments of politenefs from favages, and fhewn us that the Tree of Knowledge originally took root in the foil of ignorance; the learned Doctor, I fay, Gentlemen, has proved almoft to a *logical*, if not a *mathematical* demonftration, that Satire and Comedy, as well as Ode and Tragedy, owe their birth to the folemnization of that elegant Indian celebrity, the *savage Song-Feast*, where every man had a licence to make free with another, and to throw out jests and gibes upon his neighbour. Since therefore the Publick Orator adheres to his imitation of the great Prototypes of sublime Panegyrick, shall not TERRÆ-FILIUS be permitted to follow up the Originals of familiar Sarcasm? Shall we, Ladies and Gentlemen, be less liberal and open-hearted in our mirth than the Cherokees and the Catabaws? Shall we be exceeded in politeness by the Six Nations? And shall the savages on the Ohio and Missisippi indulge themselves in more truly-classical festivities, or elegant railleries, than the polite scholars on the banks of the Isis?

If we descend to later times, or examine the custom of more polished ages, we shall find that at all seasons of festivity and rejoicing, peculiar freedoms are allowed; nay that even some mixture of terror is often introduced, in order, as may be supposed, to give a higher relish to the other portions of the Celebrity. The Spanish bull-feasts, and old English tilts and tournaments are of this nature; or to confine my illustrations entirely within the limits of our own times and nation, and to shew we love a little horse-radish with our roast-beef, what do you think, Gentlemen and Ladies,
of

of the Champion at a Coronation? Is not a doughty knight, armed cap-a-pee, prancing in upon a milk white palfrey, by found of trumpet and beat of drum, and throwing his gauntlet in defiance, a moſt tremendous apparition? He makes his entrance too during the peaceful ceremonial of Dinner-time, yet I never heard that he frightened away the ſtomach of the moſt delicate Lord or Lady, or infuſed terror into any of the worſhipful Aldermen.—Do not let TERRÆ-FILIUS diſturb your *Gaudies*, Gentlemen!

Suffer me, then, Ladies and Gentlemen, in like manner, at this ſeaſon of general feſtivity, armed at all points, with all the accoutrements of the Old TERRÆ-FILIUS, and mounted on a high-bred Pegaſus, to make my uſual cavalcade among you. You, who have ſhewn yourſelves willing to afford general encouragement, who have committed your eyes to the care of *Chevalier* TAYLOR, and your tongues to *Profeſſor* SHERIDAN; you, who have given a hoſpitable reception to Drybutter on the Glaſſes, and Maddox on the Wire; you, who have welcomed the arrival of the Fire-Eater, and the Giant, and the Dwarf, and the Hermaphrodite; you, who have with infinite propriety circulated papers, propoſing to honour that accompliſhed Maſter

Master of *Legerdemain*, *Highman Palatine*, the HIGH-GERMAN ARTIST, with the degree of MASTER of ARTS; receive your old acquaintance TERRÆ-FILIUS! invest him with all the dignities, privileges, and immunities of his Office; let the javelin-men in rusty green, and the two cracked trumpets precede him, as they do the Judges of Assize, and let none but acknowledged felons and fore-doomed convicts be afraid of the consequences of our opening our Commission of *Oyer* and *Terminer*.

Let such delinquents however, and such it seems there are, let such I say, tremble! My arm is raised, the scourge is in my hand, and conscience (which, according to Swift, is a *pair of breeches*) lays them bare before me. Let all, to whom the lines which stand at the head of this paper, are any way applicable, prepare to be arraigned for their crimes and misdemeanors, and receive sentence *foro conscientiæ* accordingly. I will not *now* transcribe a translation of my Motto from *Francis* or *Creech*, or after the new-fangled fashion of modern wits, give a new one of my own, *adapted to modern manners*;* but I rather chuse to enforce and illustrate

the

* The mottoes to *the Connoisseur*, then not long collected and published in volumes, were the first given in that style and manner.

the alarming words of the Roman Satirist, by the following still more tremendous Quotation from Shakefpeare.

— — — — Tremble, thou Wretch,
That hast within thee undivulged Crimes,
Unwhipt of Justice! Hide thee, thou bloody Hand;
Thou Perjure, and thou Simular of Virtue,
That art incestuous: Caitiff, shake to Pieces,
That under Covert and convenient seeming,
Hast practis'd on Man's Life! Close pent-up Guilts,
Rive your concealing Continents, and ask
This dreadful Summoner Grace!   KING LEAR.

The regular difpatch of bufinefs, and the folemn adminiftration of juftice muft however, be deferred till to-morrow: To-day the edge of our Satire, like the ax before the condemnation of a State-Prifoner, fhall be turned away from the criminal. In the mean while, for the next twenty-four hours, let the Univerfity be at reft! let the *tea-giving* Belles of this town, who have danglers in fquare caps and hanging fleeves, *who boaft the triumphs of a letter'd heart*, not put the pit-a-pat-ation of their dear little bofoms into a flutter! Let the rofy Doctors and my good *Mafters* in every Common-Room fleep in peace, till their next neighbour informs them that the bottle is at their elbow! Let them fmoke their pipes in fecurity! Let not pale faces turn red, nor red faces turn pale! To-day (such is my respect for the Anniversary of the Commemoration) I will not disturb even the tranquillity of a Pot-house! Let the young Smarts, and Bucks, and Bloods of the University lay aside their apprehensions for to-day! I will not discompose their dress by remarking on an unstatutable Waistcoat or the want of a Band, or attempt to put their Hair out of *Kidney*. I will not, like an unmannerly Dean or Censor of a College, break in upon them to interrupt the evening's amusement of Cards or Dice, the brisk circulation of Toasts, or the *merry merry round* of Catches at their rooms; nor attempt to *take* them, like the Proctor, over a late bottle at the Coffee-house. I will not, like another GREAT TOM, toll them into College with a *hundred* sober hum-drum Mementoes, that it is *past nine o'Clock*; nor will I lay open the mysteries of their Scenes of Merriment in London, Woodstock, and Ladygrove: and if I fine them for their irregularities, it shall be in a much more moderate sum than Forty Shillings, or any other *Sconce* imposed by the Proctors. The Price of my Papers, Gentlemen, is no more than Sixpence apiece.

ADVERTISEMENTS

ADVERTISEMENTS.

Oxford, April 1, 1763.
IN THE PRESS,
And speedily will be published, in Two Volumes Octavo,

THE COLLEGE ATALANTIS;
OR,
SECRET HISTORY of the Chancellor, Vice-Chancellor, Heads of Houses, Proctors, Pro-Proctors, Professors, Doctors, Fellows, Students, Scholars, Servitors, Scouts, Bedmakers, &c. &c. &c. of this University:
With explanatory Notes, and a copious Index of Names and Characters.
By TERRÆ-FILIUS.

Siquis erat dignus describi, quòd malus, aut fur,
Quòd mœchus foret, aut ficarius, aut alioqui
Famosus, multâ cum libertate notabant, HOR.

Price HALF-A-GUINEA only.
Printed for James Parker, Sackville Fletcher, Daniel Clements, R. Prince, and to be had of all the Booksellers in the several Universities of Oxford, Cambridge, Aberdeen, Edinburgh, and Glasgow.

High-Street, Oxford, July 5, 1763.
PROPOSALS for Printing by SUBSCRIPTION,
In ROYAL QUARTO,

THE Proceedings of the House of CONVOCATION, with all the Original Papers respecting the Case of TERRÆ-FILIUS, Master of Arts, and Fellow of ⸺ College, in Oxford, with Academical Remarks.
By TERRÆ-FILIUS.
Price *only* One Guinea; *the Whole* to be paid at the Time of subscribing.

No more Copies will be printed than are subscrbed for, and the Names of the Subscribers will NOT printed.

TERRÆ-FILIUS.

NUMBER II.

Wednesday, July 6, 1763.

Quis novus hic nostris successit sedibus hospes?   VIRGIL.

Who is he? what's his name? a stranger guest!
Comes he in serious earnest, or in jest!

LADIES AND GENTLEMEN.

OF all the Literary Commodities, which are at present brought to market, there is not one which produces half so large a demand, or such a quick sale as SCANDAL. Formerly the sweet flowers of Poetry, like Myrtle or Orange Trees in Pots, were the chief ornaments of a Bookseller's Window, and sold as well as Roses and Hyacinths at Covent-Garden; but now every bud and blossom of Helicon, every fruit and flower of Poetry, every shrub of Parnassus is an unprofitable weed, unless

it

it be as bitter as Wormwood, or Coloquintida. Heavy Treatifes, Moral Difcourfes, and dull Differtations, were once as greatly in requeft as beef at Leaden-hall; and Religion and Philofophy were as fixt ftaple commodities as corn at Bear-Key. Law, in white Calf-fkin, while there were any *Students* in the profeffion, fold at as high rates in the purlieus of the Temple or Lincoln's Inn, as the Calf itfelf in Smithfield; and till the poring over mufty *Parchments* was exploded in the Inns of Court, the Sheep-fkin was almoft as valuable as the Sheep. It was eafy alfo for the Manufacturers of Syftems and Paradoxes to drive a kind of contraband trade in Deifm, Infidelity, and fuch other Hardware; and little Dablers in Ink often made fuccefsful cruifes in fmuggling Prophanenefs and Bawdry. In a word, every common Pedlar in a Magazine was thought to have fome curious Trinket in his Pack; and the loweft Hawker was fure to make a dinner on a Bloody Murder, or the King's Speech.

Thefe times, wherein the great Mart of Letters was in fuch a flourifhing fituation, were indeed glorious! but now, to the unfpeakable detriment of Trading Authors of almoft every denomination, Literary Property is reduced to a very narrow compafs;

compass; and the richest *Copyholders* not only groan under the load of heavy Fines and new Impositions, but see their most valuable Possessions perishing under their hands, or in spite of every fence of Law and Equity, invaded by bold trespassers from Scotland. For many parcels and whole bales of goods they have now no vent. No performance can promise itself a great run that is not highly seasoned with *Abuse*; and the nearer a Writer approaches to unquestionable Libel, and the most open *Scandalum Magnatûm*, the more his Work will be read. If a smart piece of Satire is thought to have occasioned a duel, though it is doubtful whether the pistols of the combatants ever were more than upon half-cock, the paper will run off like wild-fire. An information in the King's-Bench, or a visit from a King's Messenger will carry off a dozen impressions; and if the Author stands in the Pillory, or is committed to Newgate, or sent to the Tower, the fortune of the Bookseller is made for ever.

It is plain therefore, Ladies and Gentlemen, from these and many other considerations, which I have duly weighed and deliberated, that SCANDAL is the most profitable commodity which a Writer can deal in, being that to which Readers give the moſt encouragement. *Scandal-mongers*, like Fiſh-mongers, may put what price they pleaſe on their goods, and be ſure to have them all bought off their hands, provided they will take care to ſupply their cuſtomers freſh and freſh. *This therefore is to give Notice*, that I, TERRÆ-FILIUS, at the Univerſity-Scandal-Office in Oxford, have determined to open a ſhop in the High-Street, during the ENCÆNIA; and though all will be accounted fiſh that comes to my net, yet to avoid creating a glut, which might make my ſtock too cheap, I ſhall, like the reſt of my *honeſt fraternity*, throw away the *ſmall Fry*, and offer you nothing but the very Prime of the Market; and I can aſſure you, Ladies and Gentlemen, that I have ſeveral *odd Fiſh*, and ſuch as were never exhibited to ſale before, which are juſt *brought to town* BY LAND CARRIAGE.

I have already received, in conſequence of my late requeſt by publick advertiſement, ſeveral very curious and entertaining anecdotes concerning ſome of the moſt eminent Perſonages attending the preſent Celebrity, aliens and viſiters, as well as inhabitants and members of Colleges, with many of which, the names of the parties printed at full length, I propoſe to oblige my Readers;

reſerving

reserving the reſt to enrich the two Volumes of my *College Atalantis*, Subſcriptions. to which pour in a-pace, abundantly more than ſufficient to defray the expence of any Proſecutions which my Papers may incur, or to carry on ſuch actions as I may think neceſſary to maintain, in vindication of the Freedom of the Subject, and the Liberty of the Preſs.

But while I am thus employed in collecting materials for Secret Hiſtory, and puſhing as far as poſſible my reſearches into the characters of others, you, I find, Ladies and Gentlemen, are equally aſſiduous in your enquiries after Me. It is a well known remark of Addiſon, that Readers never entertain a true reliſh for a Performance, till they know ſomething of the Author; as whether he is a fair man, or a black man ; a ſhort, man, or a tall man ; a nobleman, or a gentleman, or a tradeſman, or a highwayman ; a divine, a lawyer, or a phyſician ; high or low ; rich or poor : ſorry am I to be obliged to call in queſtion the obſervation of ſo fine a writer, but I muſt beg leave to inſiſt on it, that till the Book is, by ſome means or other,—by its Whimſicalneſs, its Scurrility, or no matter what—become the object of general. notice, nobody cares a farthing about

about the Writer. Then, indeed, when the alarm is given, when Merit has made its way, or when Fashion or Caprice have given the nod of approbation, then the Hue and Cry goes abroad after the Author.—Who is he? which is he? where is he? what says he?—This is, and I'll be judged by Mr. Shandy,—this is, as the *Laureat* terms it, *the Honeymoon of Wit.*——Now Lords ask him to dinner; Ladies take him to Ranelagh; and Managers give him the Freedom of the Theatre. His Name is in every News-paper, and his Face in every Print-shop. If the real Author is not known, a substitute, as in the case of Militia-Men, is appointed to serve in his stead, which the world runs after with as much eagerness, as Turnus pursues the airy image of Æneas, or rather as the Booksellers pursue the phantom of an Author in the Dunciad.

I had once some thoughts, in order to gratify the reigning passion for Caricature, of having my head cut in wood, and placed at the front of these papers. At another time I had half formed a resolution of having my face painted by Haggarty, and hung up as a sign, at the door of my Printer. But finding that *masked Balls* are coming into fashion, I at last determined to mix among the

I   croud

croud in difguife, with the liberty of other Mafqueraders, of attacking every perfon in company, in a feigned voice, with the witty Interrogation of *Do you know me?*

Curiofity, however, is not to be repreft, and there are many that will flatter themfelves they fee through the difguife. They know your walk, your voice, your air, or fome little peculiarity in your manner, or deportment. I have had the honour of being miftaken for feveral celebrated perfons already, and every man is convinced that I am one of his old acquaintance. Some take me for that merry *fellow*, the facetious Author of *The Companion to the Guide, and the Guide to the Companion*; that lively fpark who fhewed early dawnings of a Poetical Genius, and foon proved himfelf a fine chopping boy, that would do honour to his ALMA MATER, when he fung *the Triumphs of Ifis:* who not only brings up the rear of *Epicædia* and *Gratulationes* with uncommon fpirit, but can alfo defcend from the fublimer exercifes of his Mufe, to celebrate the *Maker of Mutton-Pies*, or compofe *Odes on Grizzle-Wigs:* who, though now a grave Tutor, cannot furely, nay fhould not, wholly forget his days of pupilage; and though now

"– – – – the

"— — — — — the Days are come
"When calm he smokes in Common-Room,
"And dines, with Breast untroubled, under
"The Picture of the pious Founder*,"

yet he must remember the days when his ALE first became a rival to Phillips's CYDER; the days when he frequented Christ-Church, and spent his evening at Captain Jolly's.

Some there are, who suppose me to be no other than that grave Antiquarian, that SOUL OF ALL SOULS, who obliged the world some years ago with a dissertation on *the* MALLARD; who has since appeared in the shape of a Decypherer, and wrote *an Explanation of the* OXFORD ALMANACK; and about the same time, like an expert Gamester, played *my* cards most notably at a certain Game of ALL FOURS.

Others take me for that Rattle the STUDENT; and others for that Dapperwit the GENIUS; and some for both these together who have come down expresly from London, like the chairmen with their sedans; or like a pair of oars on the Thames in Whitson-Holydays, have agreed to ply together, during the present Celebrity on the Isis. Should it be the first of these wags, it is

pretended

* *Progress of Discontent—by the Rev. Mr. T. Wharton.*

pretended that the company may expect a *Sign Post Exhibition*, or that the solemn Oratorios under the direction of Dr. Hayes, the Professor of Musick will be turned into ridicule by a *grand Burlesque Ode*, and a masked Band from Ranelagh: and in case it should be the other *Little Wit*, it is supposed that, besides threatning the University with a Terræ-Filius, he means once more to convert the Tennis-Court into a Playhouse, and, in defiance of the Statute *De ludis prohibitis*, to bring down a company of Comedians *(funambulos et histriones)* to present us with new Jealous Wives, and new Polly Honeycombes, of his own composition.

Some few, who indulge this last way of thinking, are half inclined to suppose that Terræ Filius is the Haymarket Momus, who formerly *gave Tea*, and *took off* his Tutor and the rest of the Fellows at Worcester-College; in which honourable Society he is acknowledged to be a *Founder's Kin*, of which circumstance perhaps he may one day or other claim the benefit, notwithstanding the objections raised in Dr. Blackstone's learned Treatise on *Collateral Consanguinity*.

Others again, the ministerial and anti-ministerial Characters in the University, whose ideas of Wit and Humour are almoſt entirely abſorbed in Port and Politicks, will have it that I am one or other of the ſuppoſed Authors of the *North-Briton*; ſince it is generally reported that the *Reverend Gentleman*, having ſnapped the laſt cord of poor Hogarth's heart-ſtrings, will come down in his laced hat, like *General* Churchill, or Tiddy-Doll, and being a member of the Univerſity of Cambridge, it is taken for granted that the Convocation will take this publick opportunity of admitting him *ad eundem*. At the ſame time too the News-papers having already informed us that *the Member of Parliament for Ayleſbury* will be here in his way to Stowe, the Squire is hourly expected with a grand retinue of Compoſitors, Preſsmen, Devils, and *his own extempore travelling Preſs* from Great George Street, Weſtminſter.

Such, it ſeems, and ſo various, are the ſentiments of different little cabals in this Town and Univerſity, concerning the real Perſon of TERRÆ-FILIUS. Whether he be either, or neither, or one, or all of the characters abovementioned, time alone muſt diſcover. He is determined, like the Actors among the Antients, to play out his little Comedy in a Maſk, and

all

all the notification which he thinks proper to give of himself in his present *Bills*, is, that at the *particular desire of several Persons of Quality*, the part of T.ERRÆ-FILIUS is attempted by a GENTLEMAN FOR HIS OWN DIVERSION, *being the first time of his appearing in that character.*

POSTSCRIPT.

TERRÆ-FILIUS, willing, as much as in him lies, to promote a general obedience to the Programma issued from the Court of Delegates, ordering *That, During the time of this Solemnity, all Persons* COMPORT THEMSELVES *with such Sobriety and Modesty as may tend to the Reputation and Honour of the University*, begs leave to recommend the following faithful Extract from the Statute of *Quales Tutores*, &c. to the *very serious Consideration* of the grave and learned Tutors in this University.

" *Tutoris etiam muneri incumbit, quoad ea quæ ipsius oculis quotodie sese ingerere necesse est* (qualia sunt **Vestes, Ocreæ,** CAPILLITIUM, &c.) *pupillos suos intra modum a Statutis præscriptum continere; quem si excesserint Pupilli, Tutor pro primâ, secundâ et tertiâ vice quâ deliquisse Pupillus deprehensus fuerit, sex solidis & octo denariis mulctabitur:*
quartâ

quartâ verò vice Tutoris munere ipſe interdicet Vice-Cancellarius.

For the benefit of our Female Readers, and ſuch Gentlemen as have *not got,* or have *forgot* their *Latin,* is ſubjoined the following Tranſlation.

" It belongs alſo to the office of Tutor, in
" regard to thoſe things which muſt neceſſarily
" paſs daily under his very noſe (as *Cloaths, Boots,*
" HAIR, PERIWIG, *&c.*) to keep his Students
" *dreſt in the Faſhion* preſcribed by the Statutes ;
" which if the Pupils exceed, the TUTOR for
" the *firſt, ſecond,* and *third* time in which the
" Pupil ſhall be *found guilty, ſhall be* SCONCED
" *ſix Shillings and Eight-pence* ; but the *fourth*
" time the Vice-Chancellor ſhall put him out
" of the office of Tutor."

TERRÆ-FILIUS.

NUMBER III.

Thursday, July 7, 1763.

Spectatum veniunt, veniunt spectentur ut ——— OVID.

What is't, by coming here, they mean?
They come to see, and to be seen.

THE reigning passion of this nation, for some few years past, seems to have been the love of Shews, and Spectacles, and Festivals, and Solemnities. During the war, the people betrayed several symptoms of this rage after fine fights, and many thousands followed the Camp, as young ensigns often take to the army, for the sake of its splendor and gaiety. One week all the vehicles in England and from the coach and six, or landau with two postilions, down to the one horse chaise, and sober sulky, fulky, were whirling paffengers along the road from all quarters towards Portfmouth, to fee the Fleet affembled at Spithead; and the next, the fame people were tranfported with the fame rapidity, by the fame paffion for a fight and a croud, to behold the evolutions and *manœuvres* of the regiments of Militia embodied and encamped at Winchefter. At the Coronation the tide of company from every county in the kingdom flowed, like rivers difcharging themfelves into the fea, into the metropolis. Laft fummer one would have imagined that all the famous witches of Lancafhire had been at work to draw the whole city of London from its foundations, which feemed, like Birnam wood going to Dunfinane, to be all moving together to Prefton Guild. This fummer, now that Oxford is become the fcene wherein the Grand Shew is exhibited, and the doors of the Sheldonian Theatre are thrown open for almoft a whole week, it is no wonder that London once more empties itfelf into this magnificent refervoir, and that all ranks and degrees of people are affembled to fee the doctors in fcarlet, and to attend the Lectures of TERRÆ-FILIUS.

There is not a man on earth, Ladies and Gentlemen, who is a truer lover of mirth and jollity than

than myself; and I take a most particular delight in the present ENCÆNIA. It gives me an unspeakable pleasure to see the new *Dunstable-bonnets* mixt with square caps, and a gown and petticoat by the side of a gown and cassock. I could stand whole hours to see the white fustian riding-habits and blue sattin-waistcoats make their entry at East-Gate; and am transported to see the boot and the basket of all the stage-coaches filled with rosin and cat-gut, and fiddles, and hautboys, and clarionets, and french-horns, and bass-viols, while the inside and outside of every machine is crouded with the performers, English and Italian, vocal and instrumental. Festivals and Solemnities have, I grant, their uses and advantages; and far be it from me to attempt to erase any of the red-letter days from *the* OXFORD *Almanack!* It must however, at the same time be confessed, that scenes of grandeur, and seasons of celebrity, which serve merely for relaxation to the studious, and fill the intelligent mind with great ideas, often prove only new occasions of idleness to the holy-day-making tradesmen, and open nothing but the mouth of the ignorant, who stand agape, gazing with a foolish face of pleasure and astonishment. I am not one who lament as a disappointment our not having

fireworks

TERRÆ-FILIUS. Nº III.

fireworks on occasion of the present Peace; and think that the 40,000 people, assembled last week in Hyde-park, had sufficient consolation in the review. I am glad indeed to see our CHANCELLOR presiding in person, for the first time, at a publick Solemnity among us, yet do I not wish for the installation of another to produce more spectacles, though as magnificent as what we saw at the installation of Lord WESTMORLAND: and for the above reasons, as well as for some others which I do not think it prudent or advisable to mention at present, I hope it will be long, very long, before there is another Coronation!

Going along the High-street last Tuesday morning I was observing, not without a smile, one of those modern tottering crazy vehicles, half-post-chaise, half-chariot, neither one nor the other, and yet something of both, driving towards the Angel Inn-yard; but turning my eyes from the carriage to the persons it contained, whom should I see, but my good friend Mr. FOLIO the bookseller, near St. Paul's, and his wife, Mrs. FOLIO; who at that very instant happening to dart the rays of her bright eyes in right angles upon me, she pulled my Friend FOLIO by the sleeve, who seemed half a-sleep by her side. FOLIO no sooner saw me, than he ran his head and neck a yard and a half out of the chariot window, and bawled out luſtily Mr. ——— but hold, I muſt not tell my name. I followed the chariot into the Inn-yard, and had the honour of handing out Mrs. FOLIO.

The firſt ceremonies occaſioned by this our unexpected interview being over, and being quietly ſeated in the parlour, Mr. FOLIO informed me, that having a new edition of a Jeſt-Book printing at a private preſs in Oxford, he took this opportunity of viſiting the Univerſity, and giving Mrs. FOLIO an agreeable airing; after which he enquired very cordially after Mr. Fletcher of the Turle, Mr. Daniel Prince, and the reſt of his brother Bookſellers in Oxford. I find too, continued he, you have a TERRÆ-FILIUS,—a new paper I ſuppoſe,—pray who is the Author? Does it make a noiſe? Does it ſell? How many do they print? Would you be ſo kind now, my dear Sir, (taking me by the hand and ſmiling) as to aſſiſt me in making proper extracts, and furniſh me with a few occaſional paragraphs to ſend up to the Ledger, and Lloyd's Evening Poſt? To theſe various interrogations I made no other reply, than enquiring after the younger part of the family,—I hope Miſs FOLIO is well, Ma'am,—Very well Sir, I
thank

thank you, faid Mrs. Folio; we had fome thoughts of bringing her down with us, but my *fpoufe* had fuch a quantity of things to put into the chariot, that we could not eafily croud *three on us* into it: fo I have left Polly in our lodgings at Iflington Spa, and there, you know, fhe can't be *unked* for want of company,—and if fhe pleafes, fhe may go to the *Wells* every night.—And how does *young* Mr. FOLIO do?—What! *Bonus!* fays Mr. FOLIO, *Bonus* is entered in one of the colleges—He has left St. Paul's School, and is a brother gownfman of your's; at which words he rung the bell, and on the appearance of the waiter, difpatched him to ——— College for young Mafter FOLIO, defiring his company with fome particular Friends at the Angel.

Till [the return of the Meffenger Mr. FOLIO, after having difpatched another waiter to the barber's with his wig, amufed himfelf with unpacking fome parcels and valizes, which, it feems, were what had filled up Mifs FOLIO's place in the chariot. The firft he unfolded, he informed me were fome fheets of a new work of his own writing, which he propofed to publifh early in the enfuing winter. He preft me very hard to read fome particular paffages, which I evaded, pleading want of time and

and leisure to give it due attention in the present hurry and dissipation of the place.—Come, come, says he, I know you Gentlemen that write don't approve of *us in the trade* pretending to publish books of our own—but we have some *good hands* among us, I can tell you.—Oh, I know that. —Know it! Ay, but you none of you care to own it. For any thing, courtly and airy, for a Dramatick Satire, or a modern Tragedy, we have Dodsley in Pall-Mall,—Mr. Pope allowed *him* to be a good Poet—for Divinity and Morality we have Payne that lives in the Row—for Criticism, or any thing in the *Belles Lettres* way, there is R. Griffiths,—why he writes half the *Monthly Review*—and then for the whole *Circle of Sciences* there's our old Friend Mr. Newbery, at the North Door of St. Paul's—and the Author of a late Pamphlet, called *The Lives of the present Writers*, assures us for a fact that he has wrote two favourite farces.

How much farther his zeal for the honour of *the Trade* would have carried him is uncertain, if his vehemence had not been broke in upon by the return of the messenger, and the arrival of Young Folio. The mother was charmed beyond expression with his appearance in the Academical

Habit,

Habit, and vowed he was grown half a head, or elſe that dreſs made him look ſo much taller. Well, I proteſt it becomes him vaſtly? Don't it? (turning to me) you muſt know, Sir, his father intends *making on him* a Clergyman.—Ay, ay, the gown by all means! ſaid Folio—But come, Bonus! you muſt ſhew your mother and me the Univerſity——Mr. ——— I hope will favour us with his company to make *the tower* of the Colleges, and return afterwards to eat a bit of mutton with us at dinner. I accepted the invitation, and Mr. Folio having waited in his gold laced hat with a handkerchief of Mrs. Folio's about his ears, till the return of his wig, properly buſhed out and powdered, and having in the interim equipped himſelf with a full ſuit of pompadour with gold buttons, which he had brought down carefully packed between paſteboards, we ſallied out of the Angel into the High-Street *to ſee the Univerſity.*

We were no ſooner got into the ſtreet, than we were carried by a kind of inſtinct into Mr. Parker's, not only to give Mr. Folio an opportunity of ſhaking his old friend by the hand, but alſo in order to furniſh himſelf with one of Mr. Prince's *Pocket Companions,* without which

he

he declared it was impoſſible to go round the Univerſity. There, Sir, continued he applying himſelf
to me, there's another inſtance of a *Genius* in a
Bookſeller. *The Pocket Companion* is all Mr.
PRINCE's *own*,—not only his own property, but his
own writing. One of your gownſmen, indeed,
has ſince wrote a *New Guide,*—but it won't do,—
ſhaking his head,—it won't do,—much inferior
to my Friend Daniel's.

We then croſſed the way to Queen's College,
where Bonus, as FOLIO called him, informed us,
that the Eaſt ſide of the ſquare had been lately
rebuilt, and that there had been ſome ſquabbles
among the Fellows. FOLIO ſaid the Chapel was
fine, very fine, and quoted two lines out of Milton's
Spenſeroſo, for ſo he termed it, about *a dim religious
Light.* As to Mrs. FOLIO, ſhe declared that
nothing in the College pleaſed her ſo much, as the
figure over the door of *her Majeſty in a Cage.*
—But that ſhe ſaid was very pretty, and ſhe liked
it vaſtly.

We then proceeded to ALL SOULS, and the
RADCLIFF LIBRARY, at the firſt of which places
Bonus informed us, that the Common Room there
was remarkable for the beſt port in Oxford.
Some of the fellows, ſays he, have toſt off four
bottles

bottles of it a day, for several years together, without doing them any manner of harm. Folio obferved, that neither the College Library, nor the Radcliff, were as yet half fufficiently ftocked, and it would be a rare job to have the furnifhing them with books. Mrs. Folio faid, that the Radcliff was a good deal like St. Paul's, only not half fo large or fo handfome. A queer fort of building, Ma'am, faid young Bonus,—a mere pepper-box,— and there,—(pointing to the turrets of All Souls) there are the fugar-cafters.—This produced an univerfal laugh, which concluded with an exclamation of Folio's,—Well faid, Bonus! egad, I don't think that would be amifs in the new edition of the Jokes.

We then entered the Schools' Quadrangle, where Mr. Folio took upon himfelf to inform his wife that all the rudiments of learning were taught in that fpot. Here, fays he, my dear, (pointing) there are Lectures read every morning,—Here the Students attend the Profeffor of Divinity,—and here they attend the Hiftory Profeffor,—and here the Poetry Profeffor,—and here the Profeffor of Phyfick,—and here the Profeffor of Civil Law,— and fo on,—all learned men that have large falaries on purpofe to lecture their pupils in the

sciences

sciences.———Ay, says Mrs. FOLIO, it is no wonder that they have all so much *Larning*.—It is impossible to recount half their observations on the Picture-Gallery, the Bodleian Library, the Arundel Marbles, the Pomfret Collection, the Clarendon Printing-House, the Theatre, and the Museum. I can only recollect, that Mr. FOLIO met with an acquaintance among the compositors at the printing-house, with whom he entered into conversation about the method of printing *Baskerville's* Bible without wetting the sheets before they were put to press;—and that he supposed a good deal of money might be made of the M.S.S. in the *Bodley*;—that he compared the Museum to Don Saltero's Coffee-house, and that Mrs. FOLIO at going out asked the person who shew'd the room, *If there was no wax-work*.—In the rest of our circuit I remember nothing remarkable, except that Mrs. FOLIO was extremely delighted with the Bason and Mercury in the center of the great quadrangle at Christ-church, and told her husband she wished they had just such a one in the middle of their garden at Islington.

We then returned to the angel, and as soon as dinner was ended, and the cloth taken away, Well, Bonus, says FOLIO, and what hast thou learnt here?

here? Tell us some of thy studies,—come give your mother and me a *little touch* of the Mathematicks.—*Bonus*, being hard pressed, was obliged to comply; and drawing a kind of figure with his finger in the wine that was spilt on the table, uttered very gravely some incoherent jargon about A and B being equal to C and D, and parallel lines, and equilateral triangles. FOLIO and his wife observed him with infinite attention, and the most visible delight; and as soon as he had done, This, says FOLIO,—this my dear, (addressing himself to his wife) is what *we* call *Demonstration*. Sir, says Bonus, I did not think you had so good a notion of the Mathematicks.—Child, says Mrs. FOLIO, your father has a general knowledge of every thing.

Not long after I took my leave, and could not help reflecting that to people like FOLIO and his wife, Sights and Shews afford but small entertainment and no instruction: and that it would be almost sufficient for the gratification of such minds, if Grand Solemnities, were to come round, like the year of Jubilee at Rome, or the blowing of the aloe, not above once in a hundred years.

TERRÆ-FILIUS.

NUMBER VI.

Friday, July 8, 1763.

Nunc adeo si ob eam rem vobis mea vita invisa est, Æschine,
Quia anon justa injusta prorsus omnia, omnino obsequor:
Missa facio, effundite, emite, facite quod vobis lubet.
Sed si id voltis potius, quæ vos propter adolescentiam
Minus videtis, magis impense cupitis, consulitis parum,
Hæc reprehendere, et corrigere me, obsecundare in loco;
Ecce me, qui id faciam vobis. TER.

Now, therefore, if I'm odious to you, Son,
Because I'm not subservient to your humour,
In all things, right, or wrong; away with care!
Spend, squander, and do what you will!—But if,
In those affairs where youth has made you blind,
Eager, and thoughtless, you will suffer me
To counsell and correct—and in due season
Indulge you—I am at your service. COLMAN'S TERENCE.

LADIES and GENTLEMEN,

IT is necessary that TERRÆ-FILIUS, like the Senior Proctor and other great officers of this University, should make an harangue at the Time of laying down his office; but it gives me infinite

infinite concern, that on this occasion, instead of glorying in so favourable an opportunity to display my merits, I am obliged to make it my chief endeavour to wipe off a most infamous aspersion that has been thrown on my character, no less than the charge of being a Counterfeit and an Impostor. It is hard for a man on his death-bed to be put upon the proof of the reality of his existence, and though I am alive and merry, of which I hope you are all fully convinced, yet I cannot brook the thought that TERRÆ-FILIUS, should be accounted a kind of Bastard Production, (or as the lawyers term it) NULLIUS FILIUS; and that it should be in the power of Envy or Malice to make a blot in my escutcheon. I do not doubt, however, of being able to blazon my title, and to prove that I am neither an *Usurper* nor a *Pretender*.

It is true, indeed, that most of my ancestors were the most noted manufacturers of Scandal, and great wholesale dealers in Libel and *Scandalum Magnatûm*; and that in this glorious occupation they nobly sustained all the pains and inconveniences of martyrdom and persecution. I must confess that my father was expelled the University for villifying the grave and reverend heads of houses, and that my grandfather was expelled the House

of

of Commons for libelling the honourable members, and reviling the conſtitution. I cannot deny that moſt part of my family have, at divers times, had the honour of being pumped, beat, and toſt in a blanket; that many of them have lain whole months in Newgate, and ſtood in the pillory at the Royal Exchange, Temple-Bar, and Charing Croſs; and that of ſome I might even juſtly boaſt, that they were hanged for high-treaſon. I muſt own too that, for my own part, I have not trod in the ſteps of my predeceſſors; and though I am not conſcious of any ſhameful degeneracy, yet I have never been on the brink of expulſion for defamation. I have not ſo much as been taken up: I never had my houſe entered at midnight by king's meſſengers: neither I nor my printer can complain of the illegal ſeizure of our papers, or bring actions againſt the ſecretaries of ſtate for falſe impriſonment: I never had the pleaſure of having my noſe ſlit; I have as yet both my ears; and have not, according to what I have hitherto been able to diſcover, any proſpect of dying at Tyburn or Kennington-Common.

For theſe reaſons, ladies and gentlemen, as well as for the manner in which I have conducted myſelf in my office during the preſent Solemnity
I find

I find that some evil-minded persons have been induced to consider me and my writings as Spurious. They say, that I have disappointed their expectations. They complain that I have offered no affront to the Chancellor or any other person of qualaty; nor turned the senior part of the University into objects of Ridicule for the entertainment of freshmen and under-graduates. They confess that at first they were induced to conceive better hopes of me, but that it may now be said of me, as it is of the month of March, that I came in like a lion, and go out like a lamb.

These and several other circumstances, which I cannot pretend to palliate or refute, I can, however, very easily account for. A Reverend Gentleman of Exeter College, eminent in all parts of Europe for his knowledge in Hebrew, in a late contested election being accused by the opposite party of *time-serving*, very shrewdly answered, in vindication of himself and his associates, that *they did not make the times, but the times made them*. The University borrows its complection from its patrons, and the moon her light from the sun, and at a time when there is a general revolution of principles, or to (invert a little the arrangement of the phrase) when Revolution-Principles are general among us, is it any wonder that the *honest* TERRÆ-FILIUS should be as changeable as his Brethren?

I can remember the time, and indeed it is but a very little while ago, when a *place* was esteemed at Oxford as a badge of corruption, and a *green* coat the livery of servitude. I can remember too that a certain great patriot informed the House of Commons, that Oxford was *paved* with disaffection and Jacobitism. But now the old *true blue* is faced, according to the court-fashion, with *green*; and the red and white roses were not more closely twined together by the union of the houses of York and Lancaster, than the OLD and NEW INTEREST in this county by the coalition and compromise at the late election of Lord Charles Spenser and Sir James Dashwood. We have lived to see the staunch Doctor Blackstone on the point of being sent to Ireland as a Judge, and honoured with a patent of precedency and a silk gown. We have lived to see Sir Francis Dashwood created Lord Le Despenser, and appointed Chancellor of the Exchequer, and Master of the Wardrobe. Sir John Phillips it is well known is a Privy Counsellor, and our Right Honourable Chancellor is Captain of the Band of Pensioners.

Tempora

Tempora mutantur, et nos mutamur in illis.

The Tories are all at court, and Oxonians are made Bishops. The Cocoa-Tree is running a race with Arthur's towards the golden goal of St. James's; and, it is said, that at the next meeting, of the parliament a bill will be brought in for *cleaning, lighting, and* NEW-PAVING the streets of Oxford by the Right Honourable Mr. PITT.

I may be believed also when I declare, upon the *Word* and *Honour* of an AUTHOR, that it is not for want of information or materials, that I have not made my paper a *Chronique Scandaleuse*, a Journal of Defamation. I have received letters sufficient to form a volume, anecdotes without number, and satires, sonnets, epigrams, and acrosticks by wholesale. There is not a toast in the city or *environs* of Oxford, of whom I have not had a particular account; and there has not been a phaeton and four driven out of Oxford this summer, or a single excursion to Wallingford, that has not been faithfully registered in MY *black book.* One correspondent has sent me a piece, which he calls the Secret History of Ditchley; and another has transmitted an exact detail of *all* the ceremonies on opening the newly-repaired church at West-Wycomb last Sunday, together with the copy of a *carol* on the occasion, which he tells me was written by Paul Whitehead, and sung over Milk Punch in the Golden Ball. In short, so willing are all to open the sluices of Scandal, that there is not a corner of the country from which I have not been favoured with some curious articles of intelligence, with an earnest desire of their being communicated to the publick by the channel of my paper, so that had I been disposed to sit in judgment upon them, care has been taken to provide me a handsome calendar of delinquents.

A great number of correspondents have very freely and abundantly communicated their observations on the transactions of the present ENCÆNIA: some have sent me criticisms on the verses and orations delivered in the theatre; and others have commented on the voice, gesture, and deportment of the speakers, greatly lamenting that Mr. SHERIDAN, as heretofore, was not employed to instruct our young nobility and gentry in the art of elocution. One writer affects to be greatly disgusted at the vehemence and frequency of the plaudits of the *upper gallery*, bestowed indiscriminately on the Chancellor or a singer, Dr. KING or the first fiddle. Another is much offended that the pieces on this occasion are composed in no other languages

‑guages than Latin or Englifh. At fuch a time, as well as in their printed gratulations, the members of the Univerfity might be expected to fhew the extent of their learning, and we might not only, with the moſt modeſt expectation, have promifed ourſelves feveral Greek odes after the manner of Pindar, and occafional pieces of Hebrew pfalmody, but have ·flattered ourſelves with the certain hopes of feeing the elegant figure of Mr. Swinton delivering an oration in Etruſcan or Phœnician.

In this place, as I am fettling the account with my correfpondents, it is alfo proper to acknowledge the receipt of feveral remarks on the prefent ſtate of the Univerfity, and hints for its improvement. A perfon who figns himfelf *Londinenfis*, laments that the arts of politencfs, as well as the polite arts, are not taught at Oxford, and propofes that Meffieurs HART and DUKES, or at leaſt one of them, fhould be invited down to inftruct our *grown gentlemen*, thinking that he might be of as much fervice to the Univerfity, and make as brilliant a figure in that art, as Dr. Hayes in Muſick; on which confideration it might be expedient to appoint him DANCING PROFESSOR. Another perfon, a facetious clergyman of uncommon parts, who

dates

dates his letter from Lincoln College, wiſhes to ſee the intended ſcheme of a riding-houſe, (to which the profits of the laſt collection of the Clarendon papers were ſuppoſed to be appropriated) carried into immediate execution. He foreſees great advantage accruing to the church-militant, from our Doctors in Divinty being taught to ride the Great Horſe, and does not doubt but that, from their acknowledged ſkill in horſemanſhip, the Rector of his own houſe, Lincoln College, and the Preſident of Corpus Chriſti, will inſtantly be appointed joint maſters of the riding-houſe, and have the ſole direction of the *Manége*.

I have alſo received ſeveral rough draughts and curious portraits of academical characters, with the names, for fear of miſtake, at the bottom of the picture. A young buck of Chriſt Church has ſent me a cutting ſatire on a ſevere diſciplinarian, whoſe name and additions I do not think proper to mention; and a *fellow of* Trinity complains of being *forced*, with ſeveral more, to lay out an hundred pounds in taking a doctor's degree; and inveighs moſt bitterly againſt *tuft-hunters*, and a perſon whom he calls Doctor Driver.

These and ſeveral other articles of intelligence extraordinary, I have had virtue enough to ſup-
preſs

press, and think I deserve the publick thanks both of the Town and University, together with some more solid and substantial marks of their favour, for my extraordinary moderation. The affairs of the corporation are, I fear, too much perplext to make me any handsome gratuity; but, I hope, in consideration of my clemency towards them and my tenderness to their wives and daughters, at least to have the compliment of my freedom in a gold box, with a right of common on Port-Meadow. As to the University, I expect on the next publick occasion to be presented to an honorary degree, and that in the mean time, the Bursars of the several colleges will have directions to make up a purse for TERRÆ-FILIUS.

Publick writers, it is well known, have often been bought off, silenced with a bribe, or quieted with a pension, when the fears of fine, pillory, and imprisonment have had no influence over their resolutions, and all the terrors of the law have been let loose upon them in vain. Our own Times too will afford examples of writers, who, after having been disappointed of the expected Rewards from the hands of Power and Munificence, have turned from the pleasant path of Panegyrick, and gone upon the *highway* of Satire. For my own part,

being

being naturally of a benevolent difpofition, I had rather it fhould be *made worth my while* to purfue the fmooth Turnpike-Road in which I have fet out. At prefent, being the firft of my family who has not been expelled, I am refolved to take my leave in good humour, and fhall conclude my prefent Courfe of Lectures with the words in which the late worthy Bifhop of Cloyne, who had *ev'ry virtue under Heaven*, and who spent the laft part of his life amongft us, ufed often to defcribe this Univerfity.

"OXFORD is a fair city, fituated in a pleafant
"country; adorned with beautiful gardens and
"magnificent palaces; and a place where Reli-
"gion and Learning are kept in countenance."

POSTSCRIPT.

The worfhipful Sir John Fielding, Knight, and Juftice of Peace for the liberty of Weftminfter, having at fundry times not only given occafional Hints and Cautions *from the Police*, but alfo publifhed ufeful extracts and claufes from the *Penal Statutes*; TERRÆ-FILIUS, in imitation of fo great an example, thinks proper to fubjoin to this paper the following extract from the ftatutes of the Univerfity, at the fame time exhorting
the

the junior part thereof to a serious perusal of the Statute Book, that they may know the rules which at their matriculation they undertake to obey, it being a maxim of the Civil as well as Common Law, that *Ignorantia non excusat Legem.*

§. 4. *De Domibus Oppidanorum non frequentandis.*

" Statutum est quod Scholares et Graduati
" cujuscunque Generis à domibus et officinis
" oppidanorum, de die, et *presertim de nocte,*
" abstineant. Praecipue vero ab aedibus *infames*
" seu *suspectas mulieres* vel *Meretrices* alentibus,
" aut recipientibus; quarum consortio schola-
" ribus quibuscunque, sive in *privatis cameris,*
" sive in aedibus oppidanorum, prorsus inter-
" dictum est. Et si quis de die in iisdem, vel
" earum aliqua deprehensus fuerit (*nisi rationa-*
" *bilem accessus sui moraeve causam* reddiderit)
" si non graduatus sit, pro arbitrio Vice-Can-
" cellarii, vel Procuratorum, qui deprehenderint,
" castigetur. Si vero Graduatus fuerit, 3s 4d,
" pro qualibet vice Universitati mulctetur. Quod
" si quis ibidem *de Nocte* interesse deprehensus
" fuerit, poenis noctivagorum omnino subjiciatur.
" quem in finem (in subsidium Vice-Cancel-
" larii et Procuratorum) potestas sit Praefectis

aedium

"ædium domos oppidanorum intrandi; ut ex-
"plorent an aliqui è suis illis *verfentur* de Die
"vel de Nocte. Si quis vero Magiftratui vel
"Præfecto domûs, de nocte poft claufas fores
"oftium pulfanti, fores fine morâ vel tergiver-
"fatione non recluferit, pro primâ vice mulcte-
"tur 20s; fecundâ vero, commercio cum privi-
"legiatis (fi oppidanus fuerit) aliàs privilegio
"ipfi interdicatur."

END OF VOL. I.

www.ingramcontent.com/pod-product-compliance
Lightning Source LLC
Chambersburg PA
CBHW032053230426
43672CB00009B/1583